MONEY.
You Got This.

Easy to Implement Money Strategies So You
Can Take Control of Your Business Finances
and Create Your Dream Life

JUSTIN KRANE

New York

MONEY. *You Got This*

Easy to Implement Money Strategies So You Can Take Control of Your Business Finances and Create Your Dream Life

© 2017 **JUSTIN KRANE**.

Published in New York, New York, by Morgan James Publishing. Morgan James and The Entrepreneurial Publisher are trademarks of Morgan James, LLC. www.MorganJamesPublishing.com

The Morgan James Speakers Group can bring authors to your live event. For more information or to book an event visit The Morgan James Speakers Group at www.TheMorganJamesSpeakersGroup.com.

Shelfie

A free eBook edition is available with the purchase of this print book.

CLEARLY PRINT YOUR NAME ABOVE IN UPPER CASE

Instructions to claim your free eBook edition:
1. Download the Shelfie app for Android or iOS
2. Write your name in **UPPER CASE** above
3. Use the Shelfie app to submit a photo
4. Download your eBook to any device

ISBN 978-1-63047-918-3 paperback
ISBN 978-1-63047-919-0 eBook
ISBN 978-1-63047-920-6 hardcover
Library of Congress Control Number:
2015920960

Cover Design by:
John Weber

In an effort to support local communities and raise awareness and funds, Morgan James Publishing donates a percentage of all book sales for the life of each book to Habitat for Humanity Peninsula and Greater Williamsburg.

Get involved today, visit
www.MorganJamesBuilds.com

Habitat
for Humanity®
Peninsula and
Greater Williamsburg
Building Partner

To my wife, Suzanne. To my kids: Jake, Jonah, and Riley.
Thank you for all of your love. We are one.

Table of Contents

Foreword

Women Know
Birthdays by Heart

We know how much we saved on those new shoes when the sale began at Bloomingdales and exactly how many points we've earned on our Starbucks card.But when it comes to the numbers that matter most—how much money is coming in and how much is going out—many of us stumble.

(Men probably have similar money woes, but since I've spent years helping women launch careers and start businesses, I know this is true about us.)

My friend Justin Krane offers a series of mini-homilies aimed at anyone whose financial house is a mess, those who find themselves stuck in a money rut with no way out, and anyone who could use a regular money tune-up.

Take small bites and savor each nugget. You'll come away from the table with concrete steps to improve your financial picture and get your house in order. I dare you to not come away thinking a lot about your life when you read the 19 questions that Justin asks in his chapter "What xii | MONEY. *You Got This.*

If…" I bet you'll have a knowing smile when he recommends ditching the Debbie Downers who may be holding you back in business or your career.

Justin harnesses a litany of everyday occurrences (even putting on spray tan!) to prove his larger point, which is: talking about money matters can be overwhelming, but it doesn't have to be.

When you know your numbers, life is grand!

—**Tory Johnson**

Introduction

What's Up, You Rock$tar?

For the past 7 years, I have written a weekly newsletter. It's about life, money, and business.

I have this weird thing with taking everyday life experiences and finding a money lesson in it—especially for you business owners.

It has been liberating and so much fun for me. I have no idea how I come up with some of this stuff. It's pretty wacky and wild. But that's me!

So I have compiled some of my best stuff—for you!

I am so psyched you've got your hands on this book.

Sometimes money can be so overwhelming. Especially when you start to poke around online and try to teach yourself some money stuff.

You're like—what's all of this financial mumbo jumbo?!?

What are these people actually talking about?

This book is for you, the business owner, the parent, the average everyday run-of-the-mill person who is just trying to make a buck—and manage the buck you are making.

Money can be liberating. Empowering. Especially when you feel like you are in control of it, and when you use it to get what you want.

I believe you can have it all.

You can have a successful business AND a successful life.

Get the latte. Get the shoes. Go to Vegas with the guys. Give money to charity.

All of these financial gurus tell you to stop spending money. Don't get your nails done. Stop going on vacations. Eat Top Ramen noodles. Be frugal. Don't get the Starbucks coffee.

I say, GET THE COFFEE! When you spend money and buy what makes you feel good, you become happy, more productive, and then make more money.

What if you could spend your way to financial freedom? How cool would that be?

But you can't really spend all your money—or gobs of money—because then you would have none left. It has to be done in moderation.

I am all about making money—and then taking that money and paying down debt, saving for your retirement, giving to charity—whatever, baby.

So let me tell you a little bit about me, so you can understand where I am coming from.

I started out as a financial advisor at Paine Webber like in 1995.

I quickly became one of the youngest people to manage money for my clients. You know, stock and bond mutual funds. For retirement, IRA's and all of that kind of stuff.

I got up to managing about $125 million and it was fun. I made great money, I had a good office. I was exactly where I wanted to be and I was firing on all cylinders.

But I just felt like I had this freakazoid void where I was helping ultra wealthy people get wealthier. I felt like I needed to do something different and really take something that meant something to me and help people.

But I didn't know what I wanted to do. I was 29—a young little tike. Then 9/11 happened and I was in Los Angeles at the time. But I had worked at the World Trade Center for a summer in 1994.

When 9/11 happened, it really made me think and reflect on my life.

9/11 didn't impact me like it did for the families that were directly affected. But it made me really think: am I doing what I really want to do? Am I at a place where I can really help people?

And I wasn't doing my true calling—just helping people with their money. I knew that I had to leave because the Wall Street brokerage firms were all about making profits off of the clients and really not about helping the clients.

I really wanted to become a CFP, which is a Certified Financial Planner™ professional. And I did!

(Boy, it was a brutal year studying for that CFP exam.)

So I was at UBS and I knew that I had to leave, but I did nothing about it for about six years!

I was in this terrible place of fear and poverty thinking. Thinking about what could go wrong in my life.

You know how your life just changes on a dime? Because of just ONE THING. Mine was hearing this guy named Jim Stovall speak. Jim was an Olympic trainer and weightlifter who then later went blind. He travels the world giving speeches to people and he basically said, "You have the freedom to choose to do what you want."

Just hearing those words at that specific time was exactly what I needed.

So I left to start my own financial planning firm called Krane Financial Solutions.

I got mentored by financial psychologists, by therapists, by money coaches. It was amazing! I felt so good!

I was really helping people and at that time I was personally growing and advancing in my own career.

Then, all of a sudden, I just started talking with my clients about their business money. I didn't even know that I was doing it.

I just started by saying like, hey, if your business doubled, could you then buy a house, or do you feel like you're spending too much money with employees? Or, are you getting a good ROI on your investments? Or how much did you spend for that website? You can totally do it cheaper.

You know, all of these little things and then everyone was like, oh my gosh, I've been looking for you. You are exactly the person that I've been looking for.

"I don't just want help with my personal money. I also want help with my BUSINESS MONEY."

I was bridging the gap between financial advisor, bookkeeper, and CPA.

I don't do people's books. I'm not a bookkeeper. I'm not an accountant. But I understand business money—especially when it comes to financial strategies for entrepreneurs.

And I totally get how to make money.

I love teaching. I love being strategic with money and it really, really lights me up.

I'm a prosperity thinker. I am about action and implementing. So take these financial nuggets I'm going to give you and use them. Go out and do. Test. Then when things work, go big. Yay!

Your Money, Your Life—Introduction

You only live once.

So why not make the best of it?

It's not just about return on investment. It's about return on life!

Ya gotta up-level your life.

Enjoy these financial nuggets I am about to give you.

And don't forget to implement!

"Life isn't about finding yourself. Life is about creating yourself."
—George Bernard Shaw

100 Candles

100 Candles. They're yours. Your Hundredth Birthday—yikes!

How would you live your life if you knew you would live to 100?

More people are living longer.

The average life expectancy for an American is 78.

Let's play 8 questions with Uncle Justin.

They are all about living to 100 years old.

1. Would you take better care of yourself today, so that you could have the ability to travel when you are older?
2. What would your diet and exercise program look like today?
3. Would you be running the same kind of business? One where you wouldn't get burned out? What would you do differently?
4. Would you save more money, so that you could have a higher degree of certainty that you wouldn't run out of money?
5. Would you build a house that you always wanted to live in?
6. Would you pay down your debt today?
7. How would you keep your mind engaged in personally meaningful topics as you age?

8. Assuming your business is sellable, and you did sell it, what would you do after that? Really—what would you be doing on Tuesday at 10:20 a.m.?

Key takeaway: Plan for a long, rich life. Happy birthday. See ya at 100.

Become a High Performer

Are you a high performer like Mia Hamm, Kobe Bryant, or Roger Federer?

What's up with these 3? They bring it every time. They don't go through peaks and troughs. They have sustained high performance and that's what makes them champions.

They make being a high performer look so easy-peezy lemon-squeezy.

So what does it take for you to be a high performer? And how can you be a high performer on a consistent basis?

And what will it take for you to read this entire post?

Are you checking out yet? Stay with me. Read this.

Here's my list:

Meditation: I used to pooh-pooh this stuff. I thought it was for people that went off the deep end. Boy was I wrong. Talk about clearing your mind and becoming aware of what you are thinking. I am so present. In the here and now. Like right now. Meditation can make you a better thinker. Talk about business strategy. Hello!

Exercise/rejuvenation: For me, that's a massage. Once a month. Running twice a week and playing basketball once a week. What rejuvenates you? Pick one thing and do it every week.

Diet: Protein, fruits, and vegetables. These 3 work for me. Check out www.thefresh20.com for simple recipes on what you can make for yourself. My new diet has given me more energy. Major stuff for high performance.

Coaching: My grandma used to tell me, "Justin, you can't see the hump on your own back." I tell ya, she was right. Invest in coaching and get a different perspective. Better yet, invest in the results you could get through coaching. Accountability is huge. It's a great way to consistently rock the house.

Practice: Malcolm Gladwell wrote a book called *Outliers*. He said the most successful people in business who have mastered their craft have spent at least 10,000 hours learning and refining what they do. That's about 5 years if you work a 40-hour work week. Ya think he is right? Practice your stuff. Go out and shoot 15,000 free throws. You probably can become a high performer.

Key takeaway: Imagine what your life and business could be like if you performed at a higher level and it just became the new normal. You could work less and be more productive. You could make a bigger impact with the people you do business with. You could make more money. The question is, are you up to the challenge? Come on now. Forget about the whole New Year's resolution stuff. In my mind, every day is the first of January. Game on. Bring it.

Can You Hear the Waves?

I t's time to check out of the hotel. You gotta get your stuff. Call the bell guy. And print your boarding passes.

Game over. Vacation over. You just got here 3 days ago. And now you gotta go home. Talk about a major quickie.

So you say goodbye to the ocean waves. No more 80-degree weather.

You have taken so many 3-day and 4-day mini vacations.

By the time you start to relax and unwind, it's time to pack your bags and head on home.

You need a longer vacation, at least a week. Rejuvenation, baby. How about 2 weeks? Major unplugging.

You will think clearer, realize your priorities, make better decisions, and make more money. It happens all da time.

Don't even tell me that you can't afford it. Go out there and make some money. Siphon off enough pesos to pay for the vacay.

And if you think your business will fall apart if you are not there, get out of your own way!

Your business needs to be able to run WITHOUT you. Otherwise, your business isn't worth two fava beans in an old tin can. You need systems. Procedures. And people who will back you up.

So where do you want to travel to? Who would you go with? What would you do?

Key takeaway: Go explore. Go see the world. For a longer period of time.

I Changed My Way
Out of a Paper Bag

How about we take what you make in your business every year—and try to make it in ONE MONTH!

Yes! Totes. Fo shiz.

Definition of insanity? Doing the same thing over and over again and expecting a different result.

You must do something different. Otherwise, it will be the same shat different day.

You MUST change. I sat through this presentation about change. It hit home with me. MAJOR.

I feel compelled to share it with you.

It's from this professor guy James Prochaska. Check out his 6 stages of change:

Pre-contemplation: You have no intent to change. You are in total denial. People are putting pressure on you to change. You think it's too late to change. For example, you need to quit smoking, save more money, exercise, etc. You are not going to do anything.

Contemplation: You are getting around to acknowledging that you have a problem and are willing to think about what you should do to solve it. This could still take you months or years to make a decision.

Keep this in mind when a prospect you are trying to land just won't pull the trigger.

You may even know what you need to do, but you aren't ready to do it yet. For example, you know that you need to renew your gym membership and get back into an exercise routine.

Preparation: You are almost there. You will be making this change in a few weeks. You are developing an action plan and may even rehearse it. You are no longer a scaredy pants. For example: you are going to ask for a raise by the end of the year. You are going to the gym on Monday.

Action: You are taking action based on some type of game plan you developed. You are making your move and doing something about it.

Rawhide!

You are exercising regularly. You quit smoking. You set yourself up on an automatic savings plan. Go You!

Maintenance: This stage is where you need to stay in the zone, keep the same new routine, and maintain your desired level of change. It's where you need to make sure you go to the gym, check in with an accountability partner, and stay the course.

Termination: This is where the new change is so deeply rooted in your life that you don't go back to your old ways of doing what you changed. It's a new routine behavior, like balancing your checkbook every week, or stretching before and after you exercise. If you quit smoking, it's when the smell of cigarettes grosses you out.

Life is a journey and change is a constant in your life.

Key takeaway: The next time you are trying to make some type of transition, consider reviewing these 6 steps. You'll be more aware of what's going on inside your mind. You will see where you are with this change stuff. You will understand what it will take for you to get to the next level. Let's use this to change and make some money.

Did You Turn in
Your Homework?

T hat's what I always ask my kids when I see them at the end of the day.

One time, my son's homework was to pick an athlete that he wanted to write about. He immediately chose David Beckham, because we had met him the week prior. I encouraged him to write about Pele, who was an amazing soccer player. My son had never heard of Pele, so we read a little about him in the book *Heroes For My Son*.

Here's what Pele said: "Success is no accident. It is hard work, perseverance, learning, studying, sacrifice and most of all, love of what you are doing or learning to do."

It is so much easier to succeed in life when you are doing what you love. Why is it

that so many of us are not doing what we love? Did our passions change?

Have we settled in our lives and careers to just kind of float by doing mediocre stuff?

And now . . . for Justin's crazy amazing insane OMG statement. Drumroll pahleeze.

If you do what you love and if your product or service can help your people, you
will have a much better chance of achieving major success.
You guys with me or what?
Ask the Chilean miners if they are now doing what they love. How about the survivors from the Japan earthquake, or people who were given a second chance after Hurricane Katrina? Talk to a breast cancer survivor and ask her if she has a different outlook on her life.

Life can sneak up on us and catch us off guard. It did to me.

For the first 8 years in my career, I wasn't doing what I loved. And then for the next 4 years, I was aware that I needed to make a change, but did nothing about it. But I eventually made a decision to focus on doing things that made me happy.

I want to help as many entrepreneurs as possible to get a better handle on their finances so they can live better lives. It's my big why.

Key takeaway: You are put on earth to help other people and to do it in a way that makes you shine. The sun needs to shine on you.

Do You Have a
Job or a Career?

O ut with the J.O.B.
In with a CAREER. And in with YOUR BUSINESS.

I can't tell you how many financial planning sessions I have with clients where I remind them of the fact that their career should be viewed as an "asset" in their investment portfolio.

Their career is worth a shiz-ton of money.

While sometimes this asset has an intangible value, it is an important distinction in the overall planning process.

Why?

One of the biggest drivers of our wealth is not how much money we save or spend, but how much we earn and also the value of our businesses. Some people work in a career that allows them to focus on their unique abilities, which results in actions that produce tremendous results. They're just in the zone.

We often forget that we can decide how we invest our time, talents, skills, and knowledge. Really. We can. This becomes a major driving factor when measuring a "return on our financial lives."

We can't control what happens to the stock market or interest rates.

But we can plan and ultimately choose a career and a BUSINESS that makes us happy and makes us money.

Are you doing what you love to do?

Are you wearing 17 hats in your business?

Why not just do the stuff that you love and excel at?

Key takeaway: Think about your human capital. Your ability to leverage your skillset to make some serious money—and be happy while doing it. Let's go!

Do You Live Month to Month?

We just celebrated our country's independence. During the fireworks show, I got the chills listening to everyone celebrate and cheer for our country.

It's a great feeling, right? Now let me ask you this. When was the last time you celebrated your financial independence?

We all want to be financially independent. Give us some of dat. It's such a biggy.

We don't want to worry about money. We want financial freedom. We want those words and results to magically fall in our lap.

No more living month to month, client to client. We are kaputnicksville with the rat race.

This stuff doesn't happen overnight. You can't just buy a ticket and sit back and watch your own life expand. You have to take action and make it happen.

In order to get out of the rat race, you have to do the work.

Here is how you really get ahead financially:

The key is to have your assets work for you, so you aren't the one who has to do the job to produce the income. When those assets produce passive income to fund all of your living expenses, then you are financially free.

A few examples are:

Owning investment properties (real estate) that pay you $5,000 a month and your monthly living expenses are $4,000 a month.

Creating a product(s) or program(s) in your business that people can buy online and that will cover your monthly expenses.

Investing in a bond or mutual fund that pays you $4,000 a month when your expenses are $4,000 a month.

In all of these examples, you have to save money to create something that will be an income producing asset. You could also invest for growth and then convert that asset into an income producing asset when you need it.

That means spending less than you earn and saving!

Looking for a tool to track your spending? Check out my Spending-Saving Calculator. It will help you take control of your money. Go here: www.jkrane.com/mymoney. It's also in the back of the book in the resources tab.

Delayed gratification in an instant gratification world isn't easy. You have to be disciplined and pay yourself first. Automatically. Right off the top of your business revenue, not your monthly salary.

Are you financially where you want to be?

Do you even know where you want to be? If you don't, that's OK.

What is one thing you can do right now for this month to set yourself up for financial independence down the road?

Think how much better you will feel if you do something. Write it down, stick it on a piece of paper, and look at it every day.

How about a little accountability? I'm challenging you right here, to be accountable

to yourself. You can do this. I am WITH you. Why?

Because we're all in this together.

Key takeaway: You want your assets to produce the income. If that income is passive, then you are on the right track.

Funky Bedhead Breath

I t's way too early in the morning.

You hit snooze. You hit snooze again.

You pretend you have nothing going on. You convince yourself that your bedhead is so bad that even a shower, rinse, or blow dry can't tame your hair.

You get up, but then you are . . . Stuck. In. Bed.

With some funky breath.

Send someone out for coffee, tea, or a mimosa. Or maybe get a little breakfast in bed.

Now your phone is buzzing with all the things you have to do today. Your alarm goes off again. Emails and texts are coming in rapid-fire style. You already have 62 emails this morning. Everyone wants a piece of you.

You start to think what life would be like if money wasn't an issue. If you didn't have to work so hard to make money.

To support yourself. And your fam.

But money is an issue. You sometimes feel defeated by money. It limits you. Right? I'm with you. I can relate.

In the back of your mind you wonder how much money you have to save for retirement—for your future—some day when you have money in the bank. The day when you can do what you want because you have money.

Everyone wants the magic retirement calculator.

Get out of bed by figuring out how much money you could save every month.

Key takeaway: Start small. Start with anything. Get going. See how your monthly saving affects your current lifestyle. The earlier you start saving, the better. You've gotta come up with a number, one that you can achieve consistently, month in and month out. Otherwise, you will be financially stuck in bed. Once you have this number, I want you to save up for something.

Write down these 3 things:

Name of your goal
When you want to reach your goal
How much money you plan to save every month

Now use this free Fund Your Goals Calculator. It's awesome sauce. It will tell you how long it could take you to reach your goal. Check it out here: www.jkrane.com/mymoney. It's also listed in the resources tab in the back of the book.

Get the Shoes

G et the shoes. Buy your $3 latte.

You buy your $3 latte every day. So that's around $100 a month. Or maybe you spend $100 a month on a new pair of shoes. Your conscience is telling you to stop spending money on things you really don't need. Maybe your spouse is also telling you . . .

And so are all of those financial gurus on TV.

Your New Year's resolution might be to save more money. You SO want to cut back.

But it is so freakin' hard. You tried like six times last year.

Try this out . . .

Get the shoes. Buy your daily tall soy wet no foam mocha venti latte. Is that $5?

Oh well . . .

What you talkin' about, Willis?

Yep. I'm telling you to consider doing this. But you should do this under these assumptions, and if this scenario doesn't play out for you, then you will have to stop getting all those shoes and lattes.

Enter the prosperity thinker. Why not? Right?

The shoes make you feel more confident. You feel good about yourself. You feel like there is nothing that can stop you. It's a weird way of investing in you.

The coffee perks you up. It gives you that caffeine high. It's what you need to get your day started. It makes you feel good and productive.

You've heard me write about return on life. I'm all about that. But what about return on productivity? Or return on feeling good? Or return on confidence?

If you are happier, more confident, and feel good about yourself, don't ya think that you can make more money as a business owner? I totally get that happiness starts from within. But it really helps if you can make small investments in yourself to make you feel good.

Think about that for a second. Why not invest in what makes you feel good? As long as you get a great return—where you can take the money you make and save some of it for your future.

It could be coffee. Or the shoes. For me, it's a massage once a month. Or for some

people, it could be investing in a coaching program. It's about investing in yourself with something that makes you feel good.

Let's pretend that you are currently saving $200 a month for your retirement. Now let's say that some financial guru comes along and tells you, "Don't get the shoes. Don't get your daily latte." So you cut back and save an extra $100 a month for 25 years. So now you save $300 a month.

Hypothetical scenario:

$300 a month at 6% for 25 years = $207,898

$200 a month at 6% for 25 years = $138,600

So by saving an extra $100 a month you could have an extra $69 G's. That's a lot of money. That's some good stuff.

But what happens if that $100 you spend on yourself makes you an extra $500 a month in your business? Let's say that the $500 gives you an extra $150 in your personal bank account every month.

Now let's say that instead of investing $200 a month, you invest $350 a month.

So $350 a month at 6% for 25 years = $242,547.

Now we are talking. By spending an extra $100 on YOU, which could result in an extra $500 in your biz, which could bring in an extra $150 to personally invest every month, you would have an extra $34 grand in 25 years.

Here's the kicker. For those 25 years, you are getting the shoes, the coffee, the massages, the coaching, whatever. That's 25 years of fun, happiness, and a cool lifestyle.

This is how successful entrepreneurs play to win and play to live. It's how they think about money. It's how they make money. They invest in themselves. It's prosperity thinking. It's really cool stuff.

Key takeaway: Get the shoes, get your latte, get a massage, or get ya some coaching. But there needs to be a financial return, and you need to parlay some of that money you make into saving for your future. Keep calm and invest in you.

I Believe in You

I believe in you.

I believe it's all about the journey.

I believe in passive income.

I believe that money stresses people out, but it doesn't have to.

I think that money follows people that make an impact on the world.

I believe that every financial advisor should be held to a fiduciary standard when advising clients.

I believe that as a business owner you have to know your numbers.

I believe that when people align their values with their financial decisions, they have major clarity.

I believe in return on investment and return on life.

I believe successful entrepreneurs work on their businesses and work on themselves.

I believe that you don't have to have money to make money.

As I write this, I am fascinated that 3 billion new people will be internet users in the next 8 years.

I believe that every investor needs to know what rate of return they need to make to reach their goals.

I believe it's your time to create the financial life you want.

I believe that once you make money, you need to figure out how to keep it.

I believe that if you believe in your product/service, then you have a moral obligation to market it.

I believe in progress, not perfection.

Key takeaway: I believe you need to believe in something. Do your clients, customers, and prospects know what you believe in? Go out and tell them.

I Will Be Happy When . . .

I will be happy when I have $50,000 in the bank.
I will be happy when I can retire.
I will be happy when I land that new client.
I will be happy when I have more free time.
I will be happy when all of my debt is paid off.
I will be happy when I do $100,000 in sales in one month.

Sometimes we put conditions around being happy. "I will be happy when" can be an illusion.

Let's decide to be happy with what we already have first. High five on this?

Be grateful for what you already have.

For me, I am just grateful to be alive. This August, I suffered a concussion, passed out, and was rushed to the hospital in an ambulance. I didn't get to have my coffee until 11 a.m.! I am now OK.

But that day totally put things in perspective for me. It made me realize how amazing my life is right now—with what I already have. I love my family.

Being an entrepreneur totally lights me up. Helping people with their money situation is THE biggest high evah! I get to make an impact on their lives, which is priceless.

Enough about me, how about you?

What are you thankful for that you already have?

David Cameron Gikandi, one of the pioneers of wealth consciousness, wrote a book called *Happy Pocket Full of Money.* Here's what he thinks about gratitude.

"Gratitude does not need much explanation—you already know how to be grateful. Inside of you, you know how magical it is. All you now need to recognize is that every moment, person, and thing was brought to you by your own choices, thoughts, actions, and states of being. You did it."

"The world just creates itself around you so that you may experience yourself and recreate yourself. So be grateful for every moment, thing and, person—this is the best way to find yourself. Remember, what you resist persists. Gratitude negates resistance. Once you are grateful, you can look at everything clearly and see yourself."

Be happy with what you have. Then go from there.

Key takeaway: Happiness comes from within us—not how much money we have.

iPhone in Shower?

You are texting on your phone. You get in the shower. You realize you are still holding your phone.

You almost just soaked your phone. You got out in the nick of time.

You hop back in. The water is hot. You're loving the down time. You are relaxing, taking your Hollywood shower.

And then—BOOM!

You get the best idea for your business. EVER!

From inside your brain!

When you have peace and quiet, this is where the mental breakthroughs happen for you.

You already have the answers. They want to come out, you just need to slow down and let your thoughts catch up to you. The answers will come to you. And when they do, what are you going to do with them?

Before you get out and grab a towel, make a decision to take the first step.

Hire that new employee. Redo your website. Create that new product offering that you have been meaning to do.

Key takeaway: You need quiet time. Let the ideas flow. Then implement.

It's Up to Us

C an I be real for a sec? This week has been very challenging for me.
I've been writing these newsletters every week (for 5 plus years) because I want you to be super successful in your biz. Like on top of the world huge.

Like a picture of you on the cover of *Entrepreneur* magazine. I want your biz success to fund your goals. I want you to be happy.

I'm talkin' financial peace of mind happy. It totally lights me up.

Today, I'm taking a little time to step away from entrepreneur financial strategy mode because of what happened in my life this week.

This week my uncle passed away. I didn't get a chance to say goodbye to him. I felt like part of me died because he has been there with me throughout my life. Can you relate to this feeling when you lose someone?

It makes us face the fact that we are all getting older, and that it's up to us to make the best of our lives.

Brendon Burchard (speaker, author, and coach) had a near-death experience once.

He says at the end of your life, you will most likely ask yourself these 3 questions:

Did I live?
Did I love?
Did I matter?

So here we are today, looking back on our lives. Where did all of that time go? Don't you feel like it was yesterday when you were in summer camp or reading *Ramona the Pest* or *Superfudge*?

New chapters start and old ones end—sometimes when we are not ready for them. My friend Dr. Andra Brosh says that whenever we say hello to something new in our lives, we also say goodbye to something else.

These life transitions can be bittersweet.

Sometimes we have to respond to changes and sometimes we have to initiate changes.

Who likes to deal with changes when someone else makes them? At our expense?

Those changes stink. Big time. We all want a higher return on our lives. Making changes on our own terms is so much better.

Having money in the bank makes it easier for us to make some of these changes.

Why?

Because sometimes we literally have to fund them.

Financial security allows us to take advantage of opportunities that we feel are right. We can take chances and swing at pitches we want to swing at. It can buy us more precious time like taking Fridays off, going to Hawaii with our family, or doing charity work.

I'm in the trenches with you. I want us to be more conscious about the good changes we want for our lives. Let's use our money to be intentional (that means plan!) for what it is that we really want.

You might not get there in a straight line. But you can sure chip away at planning for what you want. Make a conscious decision to take one step towards getting something that you want.

Maybe it doesn't cost any money. Maybe it does.

For me, I have made the decision to finally take a vacation where I don't check email

throughout the day. It's a big change for me, a transition (Tim Ferris style) where I can take time off without having work on my mind—even though I freakin' love what I do!

Yes, I will have my staff running the business.

So, today, I'm off to Italy for 9 days. I used to live there. I can't wait to go back to a place where it's really all about adventure. Now that's my kind of change.

Why?

Because I made it and I financially planned for it. I want the same for you. If I could, I'd take you with me.

Key takeaway: When you align your financial decisions with what you want, it's such a good feeling. You're living life on purpose.

Make Memories

This week while I was driving home with my kids, we were listening to *Kidz Bop*.

It's where kids sing versions of new hit songs.

We were listening to the song "Price Tag." We were singing, clapping, eating candy, and getting crazy wild. We were together. I felt complete. I was connecting with my kids at a time that I didn't expect to. I will never forget that.

I want you to have a humungo, large, gigunda, whopping "memory bank account."

Here's the deal. You have to fill up with amazing experiences that will become memories. Some of this stuff will cost money. Some of it won't. (Ask my parents. They love to take naps.)

So why not financially plan and be intentional for the memories you want to create?

It's the greatest feeling in the world to be doing things that light you up. Especially when they are things that you have planned and saved money for.

Let's use this summer as a hypothetical example. Where have you always wanted to go? What have you always wanted to do? How much is it going to cost?

Let's pretend that you want to go to Hawaii/Caribbean for 5 days in August. That's 3 months from now. Let's plan a trip just for you. If you have a family, budget accordingly . . .

Plane flight = $500

4 nights at a hotel for $250 a night = $1,000

Food at $100 a day for 5 days = $500

Shopping = $200

Activities = $400

Rental Car/Parking = $300

Total cost for you = $2,900

So that means you need to save $1,000 a month for 3 months to go on your trip.

This may be too much for you to save. If it is, I understand. Just go on a 3-day vacation. Nix the plane flight, but treat yourself.

Want the 5-day vacation, but don't have enough money? Not sure where to start?

Key takeaway: You have 3 ways to get more of it:

1. Make the same money and spend less
2. Make more money and spend the same
3. Make more money and spend less

You pick. You have the power to choose. Plan and then go out and DO. Have fun. Live. And make memories.

My Big Stupid "Billie Jean"
Failure: The Real You

I'm in my Prius and the windows are down. I turn on my satellite radio. 80's on 8. Totally. Like for sure.

Michael Jackson's "Billie Jean" is on. MJ in da house. What a rockin' beat. I freakin' love that song.

I'm singing along and then boom! The song ends (don't you hate when you think it's the beginning of a song but it really is the end?!) and I keep singing . . .

Oh jeez. My windows were down. I was totally busted. All these teenagers were in the car next to me, laughing at me as I was still singing "Billie Jean."

And then I started laughing at myself. (Yep!) I didn't even know how vulnerable I was at that moment. The real me singing "Billie Jean." Oh man. I can even moonwalk.

So, who are you when no one is watching?

The world needs to see more of the real you. And you need to be more of the real you.

This real you is when . . .

You speak from your heart. You set goals that *really* mean something to you and you develop a real plan to get them. Like right now.

You read Gary Vaynerchuk's book, *Jab, Jab, Jab, Right Hook*, and you tell real relevant stories to your community so that you can grow your following on social media.

You start thinking about your legacy. You want to make an impact that goes way beyond you. You feel pulled to help as many people as possible in your business and you think of yourself as a total giver.

You are aware of what your parents taught you about money and make a conscious decision if your current beliefs about money are serving you.

You *really* want to save money for your future and you automate your savings. No more willy-nilly money-saving.

You know the real performance of your investment portfolio.

You know the real business numbers. Your sales, expenses, and profits.

You have been meaning to do something super cool and new in your career. You've been afraid to do it, but you take action and do it anyways because the only you, the real you, only lives once.

Key takeaway: Get wild. Get real. Get going. Get failing. Get learning.

She Survived. It Didn't Spread.

I recently had an opportunity to have dinner with a breast cancer survivor. For a relatively brief period of her life, she had no idea if she would survive. She took stock of her life and realized that there were so many things left undone and left unsaid.

The cancer went into remission and she was given a second chance to live. She totally changed her outlook on life. She did fun stuff. She drew children's pictures, took pottery classes, and went on a cruise to the Panama Canal. She learned to make the most out of every day. She even switched careers and became a docent at a museum.

Why is it that people who have these near-death experiences make dramatic life changes? They realize how fragile life can be—that it could end at a moment's notice.

If you went to the doctor and he/she told you that you have 1, 5, or 10 years to live, and that you didn't know exactly when you were going to die, how would you change your life?

Would you be in the same line of business?

Would you be doing the same stuff in your business?

What would you be doing? Who would you be with? Where would you be?

Share these answers with your spouse or friend. Write them down. Why not be intentional and do them?

Key takeaway: Take the first step towards getting more of what you want. Write down the first thing you are going to do to move closer to what you want. Now go out and make it happen.

Steve Jobs, You Taught
Me So Much

S teve,
Thank you so much for all of the things you taught me.

You taught me to be passionate and give presentations that create really awesome experiences.

You taught me to believe that even I could change the world as a financial life planner.

You brought out the creative side in me that I never knew I had.

You taught me how to be a storyteller.

You inspired me to create a vision for myself and for my clients.

In business, you taught me to never do things just for the money. You told me that "being the richest man in the cemetery doesn't matter." You told me "going to bed every night knowing you did something wonderful," is what life is all about.

And you taught me that "you can't connect the dots looking forward; you can only connect them looking backwards. So you have to trust that the dots will somehow connect in your future. You have to trust in something—your gut, destiny, life, karma, whatever. This approach has never let me down, and it has made all the difference in my life."

I look at this quote almost every single week.

I know there will come a time when my kids will come to me for advice on what they should do when they need to choose a major in college, find a job, and start their careers.

I will tell them what you taught me:

"Your work is going to fill a large part of your life, and the only way to be truly satisfied is to do what you believe is great work. And the only way to do great work is to love what you do. If you haven't found it yet, keep looking. Don't settle. As with all matters of the heart, you'll know when you find it. And, like any great relationship, it just gets better and better as the years roll on."

The Monkey Bars

For the past year, my son Jonah has watched in awe as kids older and stronger than him climbed across the monkey bars.

Jonah has tried to do it himself, but was unsuccessful, until last weekend.

Before, he could only reach out to the first bar and then he would fall down. But this time he had a little help from someone other than me—his grandfather. My father encouraged him to try and reach for the next bar, which Jonah actually did. (Do kids ever listen to their parents?)

As Jonah was successfully traversing each bar, he had the happiest face ever, and when he made it to the other side, he had a huge smile on his face. He took a chance and accomplished his goal.

Sometimes in life, and business, I find myself hanging onto the same bar, afraid to reach out to the next one. Bar #2 is my next step in life, a place for me to personally grow and change for the better.

Danaan Parry writes about traversing the bars in "The Parable of the Trapeze":

It's so hard to let go of bar #1. As I swing from bar 1 to 2, my momentum carries me to it and I know I have no other option but to catch onto the next bar. This space between each bar represents the unknown, the fear of making changes.

Isn't that what financial planning is all about? It forces us to identify what we want to change in our lives and what we need to change in order to get there. Tradeoffs and consequences force us to reach out to that next monkey bar, whether we are prepared for it or not.

In your business, change may be:

Hiring an employee
Leaving your full-time corporate job to start your own business
Raising prices
Getting office space
Buying another business
Hiring a coach

Key takeaway: Hop on the monkey bars with me. Get ready for a wild ride. It's where you will live.

The Rite Aid Grandpa

I went to Rite Aid yesterday to buy Father's Day cards. I even bought some cards for my kids to give to my dad . . .

I got into a conversation with the guy who was the cashier about being a dad. He told me he was a father and grandfather. He seemed to be in his early 70's.

He basically told me that he was working at Rite Aid because he didn't put enough money away for his retirement.

(Stay with me because I know this is important to you . . .)

He thought he would get by on Social Security and a small pension. But it wasn't enough money, so he had to go back to work.

Running out of money when we are older. It's our biggest fear. I hear it all of the time.

You must take matters into your own hands. You need a plan.

Otherwise, you could end up like the man at Rite Aid—working because you HAVE to not because YOU CHOOSE to.

RANT: I'm interested in helping you make more money in your career. Why does this get so little attention from all the other financial planners out there?

I'm not a fan of barely getting by with your money.

I'm interested in abundance. Having money to do what you want, when you want.

Hellooo! It's always about cutting back, not about expanding!

Try starting with a debt pay-down plan—especially the high interest rate debt.

Also, you must pay yourself first. If you don't, the odds go up that you could run out of money.

As a business owner, you could put away some serious cash for retirement. Like over 50k a year, based on your income.

Talk to your financial advisor and CPA about opening up a SEP IRA, a profit sharing plan, or a 401k.

Key takeaway: Having money gives you options. It's time to do something about it.

Was That You Driving?

You know those people that love to use their turn signals all the time when they drive?

They pull the car out of their own garage and start signaling to . . .

No one.

What's up with that? Hilarious.

They aren't signaling to everyone else. They are signaling to themselves. It's like turning on the right-hand signal means they are telling themselves to turn the car right.

My guess is that when they took Driver's Ed, it was instilled in them to become maniac signal users. It's now a habit for them.

I remember reading a stat that if you intentionally do something 20 times in a row, it becomes a habit.

So lemme ask you somethin'—what are your instinctive money habits that you do in your business?

Are you even intentional with your money habits? Or do you simply do nuthin'?

Being that it's the 4th of July, let's getcha some financial independence habits.

Financial independence = not having to do something to make money (like not having to work). It's when your assets generate enough income for you to live.

And one of these assets is your business.

I am talking consistent cash flow.

Here are just a few ideas of money habits you could adopt that will help you work towards financial independence:

Make decisions based on where you are with your money. Not where you think you are.

Pay yourself first from your business revenue.

Every year, do an analysis on whether you should raise prices.

Invest a set amount of money every single month—automatically.

Do tax planning twice a year with your CPA.

Every month, do an analysis of your sales and profits.

Key takeaway: Be intentional with this stuff, but not so intentional that you tell me which way you are going out of your driveway! Unless I'm inside your house!

What If . . .

1. What if you knew exactly how much money you needed to take out of your business to pay your personal expenses?
2. What if your website homepage converted prospects into clients?
3. What if you simply knew you wouldn't fail in your business? What would you do?
4. What if you actually kept reading this?!
5. What if you and your spouse were on the same page with respect to how you spend and save your money?
6. What if you became disabled and did not have disability insurance?
7. What if you figured out a way to make your business worth something? So someone could buy it from you?
8. What if you identified 3 things to be thankful for this Thanksgiving?
9. What if you had your first conversation with your kids or grandkids about money?
10. What if you called your accountant and asked him/her for any advice on how you could reduce your taxes?
11. What if you made an extra monthly mortgage payment every year?

12. What if you cleared out your garage and donated a bunch of things to your favorite charity?

13. What if you created an operations manual for your business?

14. What if you hired a bookkeeper to help you?

15. What if you brought more love into your business?

16. What if you took a vacation?

17. What if you had the money in the bank, which wouldn't force you to take on every client for the money, when you knew it wasn't a good fit?

18. What if you knew if your business should be an LLC or a corporation?

19. What if you diversified your revenue streams as a business owner?

Key takeaway: What if your "What If" was your WHAT IS?

What's Your Return on Time?

You are staying late at the office. You're working super hard at returning all of those client calls and emails and servicing your clients. You are trying to run and build a successful business.

Next thing you know, 5 years have gone by and you realize that you're still at the office.

You really haven't taken that much time for yourself.

But isn't success really about working smart with the time you have?

Check this out. Do you believe that you can make more money by working less?

What if every Monday was national "Don't Work Day," and you had a 3 day weekend?

Ever hear the saying, "busy people get more things done?"

When you have less time, you prioritize, you focus, and you have to just . . .

Get. Things. Done.

Plus, you're more efficient.

Here's a shocking statement:

You will most likely be able to do the same amount of work in less time.

You will simply be forced to be more productive. You won't let those old distractions get in your way.

No more water cooler conversations! No more surfing Facebook for hours upon hours.

And I got one mo'.

I need you to limit the amount of personal and office drama that comes into your life during the work day.

Key takeaway: We all have the same amount of time in the day. Use your time wisely. Get a return on your time.

You're Totally Avoiding Me

T he only person that can get in the way of your amazing success is . . . YOU!

Seriously.

The "how" is laid out everywhere—like a bad fart in a yoga studio.

But you gotta dig deeper. You gotta get to the "why" you do the stuff that you do.

Especially when it comes to cash money.

Axl Rose: Welcome to the inner game of business. And welcome to the jungle.

Let's start with this: "I go into avoidance with my money."

Why? You might not understand all of this financial mumbo jumbo.

Or maybe you don't really want to see where you really are with your biz money.

Maybe you feel that you simply don't deserve to have an awesome financial life.

The thing is, you do! Take it from that friend of yours that just wills her way to success—and moolah.

Key takeaway: You must have a wealth consciousness. If you avoid your money, you just avoid your path to financial independence.

Step 1: Where Are You Now?
Step 2: Where Do You Want to Be?
Step 3: What Are You Willing to Do About It?

Your Money, Your Life— Action Plan Part One

G oals. We all have some goals. Sometimes we specifically know what we want and other times we just have a general idea.

As a Financial Life Planner, I am always asking questions about my clients' goals.

Things they want to do. Places they want to travel. When they want to retire. Houses they want to buy. What they want to have for dinner, etc.

Dan Sullivan from the Strategic Coach gave me a great question to ask—and I want you to answer it.

If you were to look out two years from now and come back to today, what has to happen in your life—both personally or professionally—to make you feel like you have made progress?

Write down your answers here:

Pick one of your answers and turn it into a goal.

Use this PDF tool to figure out how much money you need to save each year to reach your goal. Go here to download the tool: www.jkrane.com/mymoney. It's also in the resources tab in the back of the book.

Every single decision you make in your life (and your business!) is either moving you closer or further away from your goal.

Your Money, Your Life— Action Plan Part Two

B efore you come up with a strategy to reach your goals, you must be a prosperity thinker.

You need to believe that you can create and manifest the financial life that you want for yourself.

Prosperity thinking is about thinking what's possible. It's having the courage to go and do. I'm talking about stuff that you have never done before. You simply just believe that you will figure things out.

David Cameron Gikandi, the author of *Happy Pocket Full of Money*, calls it a wealth consciousness.

The hardest part about prosperity thinking is staying in that mode— and when you fall into the lack mentality of poverty thinking, you get yourself back to a place of prosperity thinking.

So . . . how are you going to do this? I've got a few ideas for you.

But I want you to come up with a list that will work for you.

1. **Ditch the Debbie/Donnie Downer friends.** If you hang out with people that always bring you down, stay away from them.

You may need to just break up with them. If they are family members—even spouses—you need to have a heart-to-heart with them. A financial therapist could be a great idea.

As a business owner, one of the most important things you can do for yourself is to protect your confidence. You don't want your friends always pooh-poohing your stuff. You want cheerleaders. Join a mastermind.

2. **Meditate.** You think I'm crazy. Well. Maybe I am, but meditating has changed my life. It allows me to clear my mind and catch my thoughts. It makes me super aware of what I am thinking. I have listened to the Centerpointe method. It has been great for me.

3. **Take care of your health.** Diet. Exercise. Your body needs all the good stuff. So that you can stay in that positive mindset. You want sustained high performance, baby. Not peak performance. Peaks give you highs and lows. I'm interested in only highs!

Make a list of 3-5 things you will do . . . for YOU. So that you can be a PROSPERITY THINKER.

Your Money, Your Life—
Action Plan Part Three

D o you feel torn between paying down debt vs. putting money in your IRA? Or investing in your business vs. going on vacation?

Sometimes it's really hard to make decisions about your money.

But if you align your values with your financial decisions, it's totally easier to decide what you should do.

So here is your action plan, young Jedi: I want you to write a letter to your kids or your heirs.

Think of this as your legacy letter. It's called an ethical will.

Ethical wills have been around for over 3,000 years. They've been widely used by Jewish people who want to pass on life lessons to their heirs.

So this is a letter about your values. It's what you want to pass on about your life to your heirs.

So write one to your heirs. You could even give it to them while you are alive. This is an amazing experience.

Notice what comes from your heart. Think about what you write, from a values based perspective.

Write down your top 3 values.

Whenever you are stuck and not sure what to do, go back and refer to these key values.

You will have way more clarity. You will act with integrity and be more congruent with yourself.

Now use these values to help you make your own financial decisions. You will have way more clarity. You will act with more integrity and be congruent with yourself.

How cool is that!

Financial Planning.
It's Not an F-Word —Introduction

F inancial planning. Borrrrr-ing!

But it doesn't have to be! Because it's all about you.

It boils down to this:

Where are you today?

Where do you want to be?

What are you willing to do to get there?

It's really about change.

The biggest change you might be faced with is just taking control of your money.

As you read through this money stuff, watch yourself resisting change.

James Prochaska, a famous professor of psychology, outlines the five stages of change:

1. **Pre-contemplation:** You don't want to change. You just resist it. You don't want to think about your problem.
2. **Contemplation:** You acknowledge that you have a problem and you start to think about how to fix it.

3. **Preparation:** You are planning to make a change. But you're still not there yet.
4. **Action:** You are ready to change and do something about it.
5. **Maintenance:** You are trying to stay on track and make sure you don't have a relapse.

Remember the definition of insanity: doing the same thing over and over again and expecting different results.

More of the same equals more of the same.

It's time for you to set yourself free. I want you to know what you want and have the ability to go out and get it.

"Freedom is nothing but a chance to be better."
—Albert Camus

Is Your Money Just Sitting There?

There is fungus and mold on your money. It's been sitting there forevs.

It's kinda just been pilin' up. Why? You are beginning to make some money from your business. You are just putting it in your checking account.

You're not sure what you should do with it.

You feel like you know how to make money in your business.

But you don't know how to invest it and you're afraid to make a mistake. You know you probably should do something.

So here are some ideas.

Step 1: Keep somewhere between 3 and 12 months of living expenses in an FDIC insured money market account for emergencies.

If your business produces steady cash flow, then you may want to keep 3-6 months of living expenses in an emergency account.

But if your business income is inconsistent, then 12 months may be better.

OK, so now that you've done that and have extra money to invest . . .

Step 2: Here are your options:

Do nothing and earn between 0-1.50% in cash based on today's current rates.

Invest it and potentially earn or lose something—no guarantees. But let's say over a 15-year period you hypothetically earn between 3 and 8%.

This is where financial life planning comes in. You are investing to reach a goal.

But wait a minute! What is your goal?

Write it down. Like right now.

How much money will it cost?

Let's say you want to buy house. How much will the down payment be? Just write it down. Don't worry about the how. Yet.

Step 3: You need to be clear on why you are investing for this goal.

What would it mean to you if you reached it? Who would you be doing it with?

How would you feel if you bought that house?

Step 4: You need to come up with a set amount of money that you could invest to reach the goal. The shorter the time frame of your goal, the more conservative you need to be with your money.

The longer the time frame of your goal, the more aggressive you could be with your investments.

Step 5: Get some advice about investing. Call a fee-only financial advisor. Ask him/her about index funds.

No more fungus and mold. Let's take some action, baby!

Key takeaway: Your business success = the money you pull out of your business = the money you will use to save for a personal goal.

Did You Buy Houses as a Kid?

You totally bought houses.

Remember the game Monopoly?

You had all of the cash. You were raking in the dough. You bought properties . . . and then you built houses. You were killin' it! People would land on your properties and they would have to pay you rent. Cash money, baby!

This passive income stuff doesn't have to be pretend. It can actually happen in the real world—to you—if you are smart about it.

For your personal finances, I've got one idea for you that is right under your nose. Go look in the mirror. It says real estate.

It could be a great time to invest in real estate—especially homes. But why today? Real estate prices seem to have stabilized and mortgage rates are crazy low.

You've probably already read something about this (*Rich Dad Poor Dad*), but are you doing anything about it? I'm not talking about flipping houses. I'm talking about investing and owning property.

For the long term.

I am NOT a real estate expert. I'm a financial planner. I'm merely saying that investing in real estate could be a nice part of your overall financial plan. How cool would it be to get $5,000 a month for doing very little?

Especially as you approach retirement? You could keep your lifestyle—or even have a better one. More travelling, anyone?

Investing in real estate is all about leverage and passive income. Leverage in the sense that you are borrowing money from a bank (with the exception of your down payment) and passive income meaning that you are renting the property out to someone that is paying you.

Think about that passive income for a moment. You don't have to show up and do stuff in your business to get paid. Passive income doesn't require you to do something every single time to get paid.

Keep in mind there are risks with investing in real estate.

You can lose money if you buy a property and sell it for a loss.

There is also the risk of a renter not paying on time or if you simply can't find a renter, which means you are on the hook for the mortgage payment and other expenses.

You also will spend time being a landlord and dealing with tenants. You can farm that out too, although it could eat into your profits.

Real-world example:

You own a house and you are looking to buy another house. Maybe you want something bigger (or smaller!) or you want to move to a neighborhood with a better school district. Maybe you want a shorter commute to work.

I get this question all of the time: should I keep my current house as a rental and then just buy another house?

Here's the key thing: you need enough money for a down payment on the 2nd house.

You aren't going to sell house #1 and use your equity for the down payment on house #2. Bottom line: you need to have enough cash set aside for the down payment on house #2.

(You may be thinking, "I don't even have enough money to buy my first house! Why you talkin' about house #2? I need house #1!" It's time to start saving—either through reducing your expenses or making more money in your biz.)

So if you move from your original house, house #1 becomes an investment property. You rent out house #1. You want the rental income to cover your mortgage payment, property taxes, insurance, and maintenance. The goal is to have the rental income pay all of the expenses on house #1.

At some point down the road, voila! You have no more mortgage on house #1. Your renter has been paying your mortgage for all of those years. Now you are just collecting rental income and sitting pretty. Sweet!

That is what passive income is all about. You also have the option of raising rents, which is a great hedge on inflation.

I have interviewed a bunch of smart real estate investors. They have told me to get in the real estate game. If you're not in the game, you can't start building wealth this way. Most of them say to start small.

Your business should have some reliable predictable income that you can depend on—in case you are ever in a bind.

The smaller the property you buy, the smaller the mortgage, and the smaller the risk you are taking.

The key is not to spend more than 28% of your gross income on house stuff: mortgages, property taxes, and homeowners insurance. I have created a killer tool that you can use to figure this stuff out.

Just go to www.jkrane.com/mymoney. It's also in the back of the book in the resources tab.

Key takeaway: You don't have to be a gazillionaire to invest in real estate. You just have to have enough money for the down payment and enough money in cash reserves to cover the mortgage in case your renter flakes out. I want you to have passive income, financial independence, and not have to work so hard to make money. Consider investing in real estate. Can we get jiggy already?

Did You Hit "Reply All?"

You did it. You hit "Reply All" on the email you just sent. It went out to 7 of your clients. The message you intended to send to one person was sent to the entire group.

What if the financial advice you are getting is the "Reply All" type of advice?

It could be the media giving it to you. It could even be your financial advisor or close friend.

Here are some examples of this type of advice:

"Only contribute to your 401k so you can get the company match."

"You should not be buying bonds right now."

"Pay all of your business expenses with a business credit card, NOT a business debit card."

"Every business owner must have $2 million of liability insurance."

"Only put 20% down on a house purchase because you need a tax write-off."

You really need to be getting financial advice that is customized for you—not advice for John Q. Public. Can I get a high five on this one?

And you need to be able to understand the advice. If you don't understand it, are you really going to act on it and implement it? Probably not.

Key takeaway: You need to be getting specific, tailored advice that is solely in your best interest. After all, it's your money, not everyone in the same email chain.

P.S. These posts are not specific advice. They're meant to open up the conversation for you to have with your financial advisor.

From time to time, I will open up slots to work with me on your personal or business money. Just go to the back of the book and check out the resources section.

Did You Hit Snooze?

Y ou hit the snooze button. You hit snooze again.
You pretend you have nothing going on.

You convince yourself that your bedhead is so bad that even a shower, rinse, or blow dry can't tame your hair.

You get up, but then you are . . . Stuck. In. Bed. With some funky breath.

Just send someone out for coffee, tea, or a mimosa. Or maybe get a little breakfast in bed.

Now your phone is buzzing with all the things you have to do today. Your alarm goes off again. Emails and texts are coming in rapid-fire style.

You already have 62 emails this morning. Everyone wants a piece of you.

You start to think what life would be like if money wasn't an issue. You would have the ability to take on work that means something to you.

But money is an issue. You sometimes feel defeated by money. It limits you. Right?

I'm with you. I can relate.

In the back of your mind you wonder how much money you have to save for retirement—for your future—some day when you have money in the bank. The day when you can do what you want because you have money.

Everyone wants their business success to be the magic token that funds their future lifestyle.

Of course you have to make more money. Do more biz. Make more sales.

I'm giving you hair gel. A cup of coffee. And a stale breath mint. Right here.

Here are some examples:

More traffic to your site

A bigger email list

More sales conversations on the phone

More joint ventures

Waking up 30 minutes earlier

A 20% increase in face to face meetings with your key buyers

Key takeaway: Instead of thinking that you just have to make more money, identify 3 things that will drive sales.

Did You Pocket Dial Me?

I knew it was you. You must have sat on your phone. I heard your whole conversation. Ya know, the one where you were talking about the fact that . . .

- You don't like tuna fish
- You thought the ending to *Homeland* was great
- You had to wait for the cable guy for 6 hours over the weekend

What's going on with this pocket dialing stuff?!

It just happens automatically—without you even knowing what you are doing. You sit on your phone, touch your phone in some weird way, or maybe a draft of air comes in and then it's off to the races. Your phone just takes over and you have no idea that you are actually calling someone.

This pocket dialing stuff happens automatically and electronically. Kinda like how you should be saving money.

Automatically.

Electronically.

From your business checking account to your savings account, retirement accounts, investment accounts—somewhere else. For your future.

Check this out.

Fidelity did a New Year's resolution study back in November 2013. They surveyed 1,012 adults over the age of 18. Half were men and half were women. Average household income was $54,100. Average age was 46.

Why am I bringing up this study? Because 54% of the respondents said they were going to make a financial resolution for 2014. And of those 54%, about half of those people said that saving money for the long term was their most important new year's resolution for 2014.

Your peers are doing this stuff. Are you?

We all know that saving money for our future is important. Our peers are doing it.

In fact, last year 80% of the people that made a financial resolution to save in 2013 reached their goal (from the same Fidelity study in 2012). And they didn't have to pocket dial anyone!

It all boils down to:

- Automating your savings plan as an entrepreneur
- Taking personal responsibility to save
- Being able to follow through

Why not just start from scratch and do this? I'll bet you can be part of the 80% of the people who reach their goal in this year. Think about what's possible. More money in the bank. Financial independence. Financial security.

Key takeaway: You can do this. Step 1: Automate your money. Step 2: There is no Step 2.

Do You Double Dip?

Y a know those people that double dip? The ones that dip their chips in guacamole, take a bite, and dip the same chip back in the guacamole? What's up with those crazy cocktail party people?

We don't want their germs in our guacamole.

Don't they know about double dipping? Nope. They have no idea. Seriously. They aren't aware of what they are doing. Someone needs to tell them.

This same principle of being aware of what you do applies to so many things about your money.

If you want to get ahead in your financial life, you must be aware of what you are doing—or not doing. You need to "know what you don't know."

Holy guacamole Batman!

Start with this. Your business monthly nut.

You must know how much money you usually spend every month in your business.

Maybe your expenses are too high—like outta control high. Maybe it's not enough in some areas that bring you some fun times. So why not take a peek at where your money is going?

If you don't, you will be double dipping your way to a whole lot of nuthin'.

Once you know how much money you spend every month, you could create a savings plan for things like:

An amazing beach vacation

College for your kids

A new website

A much needed shopping spree

A home remodel

Buying some new tech stuff for your biz

Paying down some debt—especially that one credit card that just won't go away

Some guacamole for your double dipping party—everyone will have their own bowl!

One last question, if you do see someone double dipping at a party—and they are by themselves—do you call them out on double dipping?

Or just let them continue to do it and have no idea that their germs are in the guac?

Key takeaway: You either need to know what your business monthly nut is or you need to have access to your books—where you can find the number.

Do You Really Floss?

You are at the dentist. The inevitable question comes . . . "Do you floss?"

Oh man, I start fumbling my answer . . . "Yes, I do . . . I floss a few times a week. Ya know, every now and then." My buddy Will tells his dentist that he doesn't floss that much because his gums bleed. How funny is that!

How often do you floss your money?

It doesn't have to be every day! How about just 3 to 4 times a year?

Let's take retirement planning as an example. You love your business. You want to have the option to not work forever.

Here are 7 things you should think about when you floss your retirement plan:

1. **Your cash flow in retirement.** Are you retiring cold turkey? Or are you working part-time in retirement? Will Social In-Security be around? Hint: try and develop some passive income for down the road. It could help you big time.

2. **Are you living large in retirement?** Get clear on how much money you will need to live on every month. Most people think

that when they retire, their expenses will go down. Nope! That generally doesn't happen. Most of the time expenses in retirement stay the same or go up for the first 5 years.

3. **Evaluate your investment accounts.** How are they performing? Do you need to make changes and rebalance your portfolios? Are you on track to reach your retirement goal? Are you taking enough risk to grow your money? Is your money even growing?

4. **Are you going to sell your business?** How much could you sell it for? Is it even sellable? This is HUGE.

5. **Think about your house.** Do you want to have your mortgage paid off by the time you retire? Will you want to sell your house and buy a cheaper place?

6. **Will your kids be off or still on your payroll?**

7. **Your health.** You are planning to do all of these great things in retirement. But if you are not healthy enough to do them, then this is all for nothing. Is it time for you to call that nutritionist and personal trainer?

Flossing your teeth or dealing with your money may not be that much fun. But what you are doing in both cases is really deciding to take care of yourself.

It's so much better when you are the one making the decisions rather than the dentist telling you that you need a crown because you didn't floss.

Or your financial advisor telling you that you need to work another 7 years in your biz to afford the lifestyle you want in retirement.

Key takeaway: Take care of yourself first. That means your money too.

Does Your Financial Advisor Have Your Best Interests in Mind?

Working with a financial advisor can be confusing, cause nausea, white knuckles, and severe hot flashes. Maybe even a little cramping.

It's super duper important that you start out the relationship the right way with your financial advisor.

Think about this from a business perspective . . .

What you are paying for

How you are paying for it

And then what you are actually getting in return

Here's the skinny. A financial advisor can advise you in 3 different ways:

1. **Fee-only.** The advisor can be a fee-only fiduciary advisor all of the time. In this case, the advisor doesn't receive commissions or kickbacks from 3rd parties. You, the client, are the only one that pays the advisor and the advisor is legally required to put your interests first. The advisor must be totally objective and "do the right thing."

2. **A fee-based advisor** advises you for a fee. But when it comes to implementation, the advisor can put on a sales hat and try to sell you something (earning a commission). So it's not really clear to you if your advisor is wearing the sales hat or the fee hat. In this case, most people think they are getting objective advice, but that's really not the case.

3. **A commission-based advisor** is not held to the fiduciary rule. Instead, the advisor is held to the **suitability rule**. The advisor only has to recommend suitable investments for you and can put his/her interests before yours.

The cleanest way for you to work with a financial advisor is option #1. You'll get total objectivity and the fee will be in writing. It's just an easy-peezy way of doing things.

Key takeaway: Hire a fee-only financial advisor.

This Donkey Kicks Ass

I love this one about the donkey.

The donkey falls in a well. The farmer tries everything to get him out.

The farmer decides to give up and let the donkey die.

So he shovels a bunch of dirt in the well and decides to close the well up.

Every time the farmer put some dirt in the well, the donkey shook off the dirt, and he used it to climb higher and higher.

And ultimately . . . the donkey climbed out of the well.

And amazed everyone!

The donkey was determined.

Talk about perseverance. And accountability!

In business, you must be accountable to YOURSELF.

It's all about taking responsibility for your decisions and actions. It's about self-respect and taking a no-excuses approach.

It's time to get out of the well.

You want more money in the bank.

You wish you had more clients.

You wish you didn't have to work so hard to make money.

You would love your business to be able to run without you.

You feel like you are flying by the seat of your pants.

You can have all of this. Even if you don't know how.

People will teach you the how. But you are going to have to implement. And shovel some serious dirt.

You are going to have to follow through. And execute.

And be accountable along the way. To YOU.

Aim high. Climb high.

Key takeaway: The only person you need to be accountable to is YOU.

Ever Try Canceling a Gym Membership?

I t happened to me a few years ago. It was like a rite of passage, something I had to do.

I had to make the call and cancel my . . . gym membership.

It was like pulling teeth. Those gym guys made me sign some forms and charged me a termination fee. They even forgot to stop billing my credit card monthly.

I got more of a workout trying to cancel my gym membership than I did working out at the gym!

What a drag. But it's finally over.

Many of us think that making changes with our finances will require tons of time and cost us money.

But we CAN make changes quickly and do it on our own terms.

Especially in business! You are in the driver's seat. You aren't working for anyone. You're calling the shots.

The first step is to make the decision that you want a better financial life. It's about being a prosperity thinker.

Believing you can create and manifest the financial life you want for yourself.

You must take action. Cancel the gym membership. Be HUGE.

Key takeaway: You can't steer a parked car. You must drive with your foot on the accelerator. Get moving.

Hey Snooki, One Day You'll Be Fahklempt

You are hot now, but you may not be making good money in a few years. You could be the next Erik Estrada, Milli Vanilli, or MC Hammer.

What happens if you are peaking in your career right now?

What if you no longer make $30,000 an episode from *Jersey Shore*?

What if you lose your tan and big hair?

And . . . what's your plan to have a financially secure retirement?

Snooks, the problem is that you don't have all of the answers right now. You don't have a crystal ball.

You need to be asking yourself, "What can I do right now to give me the best chance of reaching my goals in the future?" You need to have a retirement plan based on a high probability of getting what you want.

Here is what you should think about first for planning your retirement:

How much money will you need to cover your basic living expenses? Including your tanning habit?

How much money would you need to cover things that are beyond your basic needs? Like travel, shopping, etc.?

How much money would you need to cover your wishes, like owning a tanning salon (for your orange tan) or buying a vacation home?

And here is what I would do second:

Write this down: how much money do you think you are going to make over the next 5, 10, and 15 years?

Are you overspending today? (For those of you who read my newsletters, you know I believe in having a healthy balance between spending and saving.)

How much money do you need to earn in your investment portfolio so that you can maintain your lifestyle?

When do you want to retire? And will you be getting a pension or working part-time in retirement?

Snooki, you are probably getting a little overwhelmed (fahklempt) with all of these questions.

Do this in baby steps. It's like building a baseline tan before you want to get real tan.

Get tan with a retirement plan.

Key takeaway: Build your retirement plan one step at a time. Even if it takes baby steps.

Holy Taxes Batman!

We have a crazy big deficit. How is our government going to deal with this? It's simple: cut spending and raise revenue.

I've got news for you, Batman. The Joker and Penguin are going to raise tax rates sometime down the road.

Maybe they will be higher when you retire and lay down your cape.

Even if you fall into a lower rate when you retire, tax rates might be higher.

That means you'll have to take even more out of your IRA to fund your Batcave lifestyle. And because of that, you need to think about diversifying your current and future tax liabilities.

Stay with me, Batman. Lemme explain. And bring in Robin to take notes.

One way to do this is to fund a Roth IRA or convert your IRA to a Roth.

You are funding a Roth with after tax dollars. That means if you convert an IRA to a Roth, you have to pay taxes at your ordinary income tax bracket today, for a tradeoff of tax-free growth forever, in a Roth.

Do you know how many Bat-Phones you could buy with a fat Roth IRA?

And if tax rates are higher, say at 50%, you will be super set. The younger you are, the more this makes sense.

Feeling nauseous about all of this tax stuff? Don't worry. I am too.

Key takeaway: Consider funding a Roth IRA, your 401k, and a regular investment account. That way, you will be diversified from a tax standpoint based on all of the different tax scenarios. Run this stuff by your CPA. Especially when you do your tax planning. Now that is a Bat-Plan.

I Probably Shouldn't
Be Telling You This

I t took me over 2 years to watch one season of *CSI* even though I had all of the episodes on my DVR.

I would usually turn on the TV around 9:30 p.m. and within 15 minutes—boom! I would just pass out and fall asleep. For 2 years this went on . . .

Until Walter White, Jesse Pinkman, Tuco Salamanca, and Gus Fring entered my world.

It took me about 5 weeks to finish the ENTIRE series of *Breaking Bad*. That show was INSANE. Talk about entertainment. It totally kept my attention.

RANT: So many people in Wall Street and many personal finance gurus are SO boring. Talk about watching paint dry!

Do they even know that people check out after like 20 seconds if the content isn't SOMEWHAT ENTERTAINING?

This country needs *way* better financial literacy. But the DELIVERY needs to be exciting, enticing, and entertaining so that YOU GUYS—MY PEEPS—can consume the info.

And make mucho progress with your financial SHIZ-ness.

Accountants! Bookkeepers! Financial planners—and any other money gurus—if you're reading this, PAHLEEZE give your peeps bite-sized nuggets of info. Things that they can do right away. And act on.

Capeesh?

No more brochures with a bunch of financial legalese bullshat. Do people even read that stuff anyway? Take off the stuffy suit. Put on a t-shirt and jeans. Be real.

Guys, I want you to FEEL engaged when it comes to planning your money life. It should be rewarding, uplifting, and fun.

That way, the next time you look at your profit-loss statement, plan your taxes, or deal with your IRA, you will be engaged and understand your money shiz-ness.

Key takeaway: We need this money stuff to be more FUN. Yep. Fun.

I'm Not Good with Money

I hear it all of the time. "I stink at dealing with money." "I feel so defeated about my financial situation."

"I just avoid looking at my profit-loss statement."

How cool would it be if you were better with your money? Like you are killin' it with your money sitch? Like right now. Literally while you are reading this.

It starts with the stuff that's inside your keppy (Yiddish for "head"). What if you thought you were good with money? Yep. What if you just made the decision that you are bright and that you could get better with money?

Or that you could get help and figure this money shiz-ness out.

Stay with me . . . I think I'm onto something.

Your job isn't supposed to be a money expert. Your job is to make the decision right now that you will start from scratch and learn a little bit about money every day.

That way, you can get ahead in your financial life. I'm talking awareness, baby.

I read this on a blog today and it totally resonated with me:

"Hey, Money. I don't want to talk about you, look at you, or pay attention to you, but I want you. In fact, I want you to be with me more SO I can pay less attention to you. I don't want anyone to know how much I think about you, Money. Come. Be with me."

It's time for you to start dating your money. Go out for cocktails, tapas, the whole deal. Hang out with your money for a bit. Get to know your money.

That means you need to know:

- How much money you make
- How much money you have
- How much money you owe
- How much money you can save

I want you to be aware of 2 main things when you learn about money:

1. **Your mindset.** You need to believe that you can get better. That way, you will be open to receiving and learning really strategic money stuff. It's time to go from scarcity to abundance. That starts with valuing who you are. Believe that you are an amazing entrepreneur. Feel that you are worth the big bucks that people will be paying you. Did I mention that you are amazing? People need to see your awesome-sauce.

2. **Strategies.** This is the stuff I write about for the Krane Financial Solutions community. I am all about strategy. Lemme just give you one right now: automate your money. Especially in your business. Set up electronic fund transfers to wherever you want the money to go.

Key takeaway: It's time for you to write a new money story for yourself. Like right now. Having money is a means to enable you to do what you want. You are good with money. Get to know your money. It has a crush on you. Vino style. Tapas style. The whole deal.

Invest in Your Business or Your Retirement Account?

S hould you invest in your business or invest for retirement?
I get this question all the time from business owners about where to invest.

My simple shpiel? You have to do both.

Then I hear this from other clients: "Justin, I feel like I have no control over what happens to the stock market! I'd rather just put my money back into my business."

I get it. I feel your sense of having more control in your business.

But . . .

You still need to diversify. You can't put all of your eggs in one basket and only invest in your business—even if you think your biz will be worth tons down the road.

Here's why. Let's say you regularly invest in your business for many years. So the value of your business is the only thing you have set aside for retirement. But what happens if you can't sell your biz for the amount you want? Or even worse, what if it is worth zero by the time you try to sell it?

You will be kaput. We don't want that.

But what if you could develop an investment plan that wasn't just tied to the stock market? Woohoo! Now we are talking. Wondering how to do that? Email me.

So how do you do both? Consider reinvesting 5-10% of your revenue back into your business. Try saving 5-10% of your revenue for retirement.

To save, you need to set up a system and it needs to be automated. Not the willy-nilly stuff where you do manual transfers from your business account to your savings account every month or two.

We need to take things to Def Con 4 (who saw *WarGames*?). Take more control and automate your savings.

One of the first types of accounts you may want to set up for retirement is a Roth IRA. You fund it with after tax dollars. It grows tax deferred and as long as you keep it in until you are 59 ½, the money you take out is tax-free. Saweet!

If you make over a certain amount of money, you will not qualify to contribute to a Roth IRA. Go here to see if you qualify: https://www.irs.gov/Retirement-Plans/Roth-IRAs

If you want to invest in your business, there are so many ways to do it. Hire employees. Get office space. Redo your website. Or invest in marketing and technology. Your ROI could be big here.

Key takeaway: Diversify your investments. Put money away for retirement in IRA's and 401k's, AND invest in your business.

Jeez Charlie, Pull Yourself Together

H ey, Charlie Sheen.

You want to get a handle on your finances? I've got news for you, Charlie. You are going to have to put your wild side on hold and get a grip on your emotions, especially when it comes to investing and taking risks.

Your portfolio can't be as volatile as your temper.

You're making good money, so shoot for moderate returns (take a moderate level of risk). That way, when the volatility comes, you won't freak out and make a rash decision that really isn't in your best interest.

Here are 4 things to do with your money so the next time you go off the deep end, you won't take your portfolio down with you:

1. **Ask yourself** how much money, that's dollars, cash, you are willing to lose. On paper. It's all about your tolerance for risk.

    Losing on paper means investing money and seeing a loss on your statement. It means sitting with that loss and riding it out until it becomes a profit.

    Once you know this number, tell it to your financial advisors. That way, they can structure a portfolio that could keep you in the game of investing—especially when you freak out and do cray-zee stuff.

2. **Put 1-2 years of living expenses in an FDIC insured money market account.** So if your career dries up for a year or two, you will have money in the bank on which to live.

3. **Buy municipal bonds.** Your net worth is like $85 million (celebritynetworth.com)!

   Holy smokes! The interest from munis is federally tax-free.

   If you buy munis issued from the state that you live in, the interest is also state tax-free. I bet taxes are a big issue due to all of that money you make. Ask your accountant.

   Even if bonds aren't the best place to be right now (due to low interest rates), if you buy individual bonds and hold them to maturity (and the issuer does not default), you are going to get your money back. Review this with your financial advisor.

   Sometimes investing is about the return of your money rather than the return on your money.

4. **Do not watch CNBC and look at your portfolio every single day.**

   This is too much for you, Charlie. Your emotions can be all over the place.

   The less often you listen to the news, the longer term perspective you will have when it comes to your investments.

Señor Chuck.

Think about some of the greatest investors of our time. What do they have in common?

They have remained patient, level headed, and have had a long-term perspective.

They have an investment plan that is well thought out.

It's time to get to work, Charlie. Take a Valium. Some melatonin. A sedative. Meditate. Do some yoga. Maybe some breathing exercises.

Key takeaway: Once you're in this level-headed state, it will be easier to get a handle on your money.

Kanye West Ate the Bling

That's right. Kanye West put diamonds on the bottom row of his teeth.

http://twitpic.com/2afcoa

Kanye has had his share of controversies over the last few years. I bet if you asked him what he likes to buy with his money, he'd probably tell you, "Experiences and things."

He bought the bling and it also gave him the experience of getting right back in the limelight—the media, the attention, the hype.

So what do you like to buy with your money? Experiences or things?

What kind of things do you like to buy? Jewelry, electronic gadgets, cars, clothes, things for your home?

How about experiences? Laker games, traveling to places you've never seen,

Disneyland with your kids, flying your out-of-town family in for Thanksgiving?

Key takeaway: Once you have a better understanding of how you like to spend your money, you will have such greater clarity on making financial decisions. Especially with your non-business money. Your personal moolah.

You will have an easier time developing a spending and savings plan that works for you. Notice I didn't call it a budget. That's the "B" word, which signifies that we can't spend any money today and just have to save for retirement so we can live the life we want to when we are 82. How about spending some money on a little fun for today? Experiences or things—take your pick. It's all good.

Mick Jagga Has the Swagga

M ick.

There aren't that many women who don't love the guy. This guy has all the moves. He is smooth. He's a stud. But most of all, he really exudes confidence.

Mick got me thinking. The one quality that entrepreneurs must have is confidence.

So, what's your rate for return on your confidence? The higher it is, the more you will get what you want.

Once you get that confidence, you need to protect it, big time. Hang with people who will be your cheerleaders and supporters. Celebrate your successes with them.

And when you have the mojo, you become unstoppable.

Ya gotta dance like Mick.

Keeping and maintaining that momentum is huge. When you take massive action while you are confident, the sky is the limit. Failure doesn't even enter your mind.

You think Mick second guesses his dance moves?

Think of the type of business person you are when you are confident. You don't even think twice when you do business. Things come naturally for you. To be confident, you have to believe in you and the product or service that you offer.

If you don't believe in it, then why should your customers?

Key takeaway: Do whatever it takes to be and feel confident. It will make you more charismatic in business.

Money Floaties

You are done with your day job. You can't stand it anymore. You are underpaid.

Nothing gets done right at your company. It's a total mess.

You want to bail. Cold turkey. Just quit. Enough is enough.

You want to make your side business your REAL BUSINESS. It's time to jump in the pool.

But you don't have your floaties. No safety net.

I see so many people quit their day job to start a business and they forget about the money.

Breaking free from your day job and having blind faith that the money will magically show up is a recipe for disaster.

Why?

- It ends up costing more money to start a new business.
- It sometimes takes longer to bring in the sales than you thought you would.

There are so many times in life where you just dive into the pool. With no floaties. When you don't even know how to swim.

The thing is, when you want to make a huge life change, you don't have to take huge financial risks.

Get those floaties on and take small risks. Consistently. Aquaman.

Key takeaway: It is so much easier to make a business or career change when you have money coming in. It's all about cash flow.

Here's what to do when you want to quit your job and start a business:

Build your new business at nights and weekends while you are getting paid from corporate.

Don't quit your day job until you have enough money saved up to fund your living expenses for a while. Maybe 6 months or more.

Don't quit your day job until you have SALES. Consistent sales. Where you can at least pay 50-75% of your monthly living expenses. Assuming you have saved 6-12 months of living expenses in the bank.

It's OK to wear the floaties. They really do look good on you. They will keep you above water.

Poop in Soup

T homas Edison, one of the most famous inventors of all time.
He had this thing about how he hired his associates. He would give them a bowl of soup.

If they added salt or pepper to the soup before tasting it, he wouldn't hire them.

He didn't want anyone making too many assumptions.

Assumptions rule out that there could be poop in da soup.

As business owners, we can't make assumptions that there is a bunch of poop in the soup.

We have to test stuff out. We have to know what is going on.

This is one of the key drivers that make businesses fail.

According to the SBA (Small Business Administration):

30% of small businesses go out of business within 2 years
50% of small businesses fail within 5 years

There are so many reasons why small businesses fail:

No unique selling proposition

Bad messaging
Challenging business model

Those are all good, but in my heart of hearts, the reason why small businesses fail AFTER 2 years is:

Lack of financial clarity.

We start a business based on an idea. We just run with it. But as our business grows, there are so many more moving parts to manage.

And one of them is dealing with our business money.

We make decisions based on what we think is happening, but is what we think is happening really happening?

It's all about our assumptions.

Do we even want to get on the scale to see how much we weigh?

Do we even want to look at our numbers? To see reality?

Key takeaway: When we know our numbers, the world changes. It's easier to make decisions.

Should Guys Color
Their Own Hair?

I've seen some really bad hair color jobs by guys.

The top of their hair is gray. The part by their ears is a dark brown and their goatee is brown with gray.

Talk about paint by numbers! Oy. What a mess. It's really not working.

So should guys do their own hair coloring? Should they buy those hair color kits for men at Rite Aid, CVS, or Duane Reade? Should they do their own tin foil? Whatcha think?

I think if they want to do it on their own, that's fine. But they just need a little guidance and perspective on how to get it right. They need someone to show them a few times how to do it. Or if they don't want to do it themselves, they should pay a professional.

If the hair color guys do this stuff haphazardly—a little here, and a little there—they are just going to get a so-so result.

My hair coloring for guys shpiel is the same as my money shpiel.

You can do all of your money stuff on your own. You can learn and do your own financial planning, but you have to be 100% committed to learning and figuring this financial stuff out—a little bit at a time.

But . . .

It's way easier to have someone show you the ropes, meaning breaking down complex financial mumbo jumbo, giving you their perspective, and teaching you the "how."

As you begin to understand more and more about your financial situation, you will have the tools and knowledge to take some serious action. I'm talking going to the moon.

So here is my advice to the bad hair color guys who need a financial plan and, ladies, you can learn something from this . . .

1. These guys are afraid to walk into a salon and have other people see that they have been coloring their hair. Maybe it's also hard for them to be vulnerable and have someone else look at their money. They have tried to color their own hair with no help—and for some reason it just doesn't look good. They gotta let their hair down! Ba dump bump.

    Lesson: It's OK to get help. Make the decision that it is OK to be financially vulnerable. Call your CPA, bookkeeper, and financial planner. Ask them to explain to you how your business did this year vs. last year. Get clear on your financial numbers.

2. The bad hair color guys don't have enough pride or value themselves enough to look really good. They think they are stuck with their mediocre hair! These guys need to make a stand for who they are and believe that they can have amazing hair! It's all about the hair. Right?

    Lesson: Take pride in you and own your worth! You are worth a gazillion dollars and so is your business. Be 100% committed to playing a bigger game in your business. Did I mention that you are the real deal?

    When was the last time you raised prices? I need you to create a premium priced offering. Way higher than what you have today. Maybe 10-20% of your peeps will buy it because they see the value in what you are offering. The thing is, do you?

3. They don't even know that they could do better, because they aren't getting any feedback. Some of their friends want to tell them how bad their hair is, but they are afraid to. Maybe they even have bad breath or food in their teeth! I bet some of them don't know if their financial situation is good or bad because they never get any feedback as to what they can do to make things better.

Lesson: Pahleeze join a mastermind. You want a game changer? Give feedback, get feedback. Be accountable. Share your goals. Get supported.

You have no freakin' idea how much progress you will make if you join a mastermind. I practically doubled my business since I joined one. And I am on track to double my business again. So could you. You just need to be committed to the right mastermind group.

4. They don't have a paint by numbers hair color plan. I mean, shouldn't the goatee and all of their hair be the same color? It's the same thing with money. Step one: do this, step two: do this, step three, etc. A hypothetical example could be: invest $500 a month in your business and hire an assistant.

Take the increase in your free time to go out and do some serious networking to bring in business. As you bring in more clients, raise your rates. Take the increase in sales and make an extra $300 payment towards your mortgage. Rinse and repeat.

Key takeaway: You need an overall financial plan. You need to know how much you should save and where the money should go. Consider talking with a Certified Financial Planner™ professional.

Should Jan Brady
Get a Spray Tan?

J an Brady. She was tired of being the middle blonde girl in the fam. Jan
wanted to stand out.

She bought that funky black wig. It totally didn't go.

What if she got a spray tan instead? Did they even have those back
then? I bet that her spray tan would have been too splotchy. It totally
would have worked on Marsha, though. Right?

Are you into spray tanning? Some people love it, but they only do it
for a special occasion—like spring break or a vacay with the fam.

Some people don't want to spend the $50-100 to get it. Plus, it only
lasts like a week or so. Then it's kaput.

Some people think it looks too fake and they just won't go there.
Others don't want to stand naked in front of some stranger and get blasted
with cold stuff.

The thing is, if you want that year-long tan, you can't get a spray tan
just once. You need to go every week or so. It's work. It takes time.

This spray tan issue is the same deal with your business numbers. You
can't just spray tan your money for a special occasion or once a year.

Key takeaway: You have to spray tan your money every month. That means reviewing your sales and profits. It means making sure you are making the kind of money you want to. It means blocking time to look at your moolah.

Ya gotta stay on top of your numbers—throughout the year. Otherwise, you will have a splotchy money life. Spray tan your business every month. Give it that orange money glow.

Special bonus! Want even more ideas for your biz? Grab my free CD. Go to www.jkrane.com/mymoney. It's also in the resources page at the back of the book. It's about business strategies and your mindset. All centered around your life. You're going to love it.

Too Hot or Cold?

You get in your shower at a hotel. You turn the water on and it is crazy hot.

You turn the knob the other way—and it gets even hotter?

You can't figure out which way is hot and which is cold.

Next thing you know, it's been 10 minutes, you're still in the shower, and all you have is a bunch of steam and no cold water!

Ya gettin' burned up in there. It's ya own private steam room.

There is no trend either way with that crazy water temp.

Let's talk about trends fo' a sec. Your money trends.

When you make money in your business, do you . . .

Spend more? Or save more?

What's your intention? What's your plan? To spend more when you make more? Or to save the extra money?

I'm all for doing what you want. Spending, saving, whatevs, baby. But do you even know what you want to do?

Key takeaway: I've looked at so many people's money spending habits and many people spend more when they make more—and are always playing catch-up. They try to get back on track to get back on track. They never figure out the water temp. They take a bath with their money. Simply spend less than you make.

Was Your Phone on Vibrate?

Your phone is supposed to be on vibrate.
But it isn't.

It rings during a movie at the movie theater. It startles you and you spill your peanut M&M's all over the place. You can hear them rolling down the floor. People are turning around, giving you nasty looks.

Your phone freaked you out. Really surprised you.

Are you always in reactive mode with your money? Feeling surprised all the time?

Especially in your business?

Does this happen to you?

Your CPA calls and tells you that you owe $10,000 in taxes because you made no estimated tax payments.

You forgot to fund your IRA and it's past the deadline.

You thought you made way more money in your business, but you didn't.

The IRS audits you and tells you that the person you hired and classified as an independent contractor was really an employee and now you owe payroll taxes and penalties.

Key takeaway: The ONE THING you need in your business is clarity. Especially with your money.

1. Where are you today?
2. Where do you want to be?
3. What are you willing to do to get there?

The only way you can be surprised is if you aren't expecting something to happen. Or, if you just keep your head in the sand and you don't know what's going on. I believe you are smart enough to cut down on the surprises. Remind yourself that your ringer is on.

Weight Watchers Your Money

These Weight Watchers guys are killing it. They are on fire. They are doing some serious biz-ness.

They could teach you so much about your money. Here are 6 things you can learn from them:

1. **Their point system rocks!** It keeps you in check and provides flexibility. You can eat some foods that you love just as long as you don't go over the allotted points per day. Develop a saving and spending plan that will give you some wiggle room when it comes to budgeting your personal money, but don't go overboard. There does need to be a limit based on how much you can spend today, so there is money set aside for tomorrow.

2. **The weight-loss meetings provide accountability, support, and a safe place** for people to receive coaching. People can share confidential feelings about their weight and overall struggles with dieting. Hire a financial planner to give you the education, guidance, and support. A financial planner can be that neutral 3rd party. Especially when it comes to talking about money with your spouse.

3. **Losing weight takes time and doesn't happen overnight.** People who lose weight on Weight Watchers are committed and usually make progress with their dieting every few weeks. Moreover, a change in behavior over the long term keeps the weight off. Making money in your business doesn't happen overnight. It's usually about implementing a well thought out marketing plan.

4. **Once people get started** on Weight Watchers, they begin to feel better about themselves because they are taking control of their lives. Many of us struggle on the inside when we deal with our moolah. We freak out. We don't know where to start. We're afraid to take the first step. Take baby steps when planning your finances. Do a little bit every month. You'll look back and say, "Jeez! Look how far I've come!"

5. **Dietary programs can be customized** for people based on their individualized needs, so they can eat what they like, when they like it, and also eat what's right for their body. You are unique, different, and have your own special sauce. You could be an entrepreneur, a single mom, married with kids, or retired. Develop a financial plan that works for you based on your own circumstances. Not someone else's.

6. **The Weight Watchers website is user friendly,** has many resources for their clients, and provides information that lets their clients learn about dieting. One of the most common things I hear is, "I wish I knew more about money. I want to make better financial decisions with my business money."

Educate yourself. Learn a little bit every day. Read. Then do.

Go to my YouTube channel and subscribe. It's at www.jkrane.com/youtube. All the details are on the resources page in the back of the book. It's time to have some fun while you learn about money!

Key takeaway: It's not just about return on investment. It's about return on life. Merge your money with your life. Not someone else's. And make sure it's a balanced life!

Were You the
Banker in Monopoly?

E ver play Monopoly as a kid? Were you the banker?
You know, the one who was in charge of the money? Didn't you feel empowered and good? I loved being the banker. Maybe that was the writing on the wall for my future career as a Certified Financial Planner™ professional.

But today, I am not THE banker. I just have personal and business accounts at my bank. And lemme tell ya, dealing with banks today is a major pain in the you-know-what.

Calling the 800 number to get a question answered, or to get a loan, is like pulling teeth. I'm feeling nauseous just writing about it. In fact, hold on. I'm getting a paper bag. Ugh!

I am declaring today "Everybody Form a Relationship with a Banker Day!"

Even if you think you don't need anything from your bank right now, at some point, you may need a line of credit or a loan for your business. Or you may need to wire funds on a moment's notice.

Key takeaway: Whatever the issue, it's so much better to have an existing relationship with a banker—someone you can hold accountable for getting the job done for you. And by the way, there are bankers out there who are actually looking for new clients! As an independent financial planner, these bankers call on me from time to time and are looking for new business. Start playing your own game of Monopoly and find a banker. Take back control of your financial life and don't forget to collect $200 when you pass GO! Let's get to work.

What Is Yoda's Retirement Plan?

Remember Yoda? The short little bald guy in *Star Wars*? He lived for 900 years!

What did that guy eat for breakfast? Wheaties? Kale? Thin Mint Girl Scout cookies?

He must've had great genes (Levi's, True Religion, 7 for All Mankind). He also probably meditated, exercised, and took some serious supplements.

Ya think Yoda ran out of money? How much money did he have in his 401k? Do you think he put enough money away as a business owner?

What if you live a lot longer than you think you will?

In 1980, the average life expectancy was 73 years old. Today it's 78 (source: National Center for Health Statistics). I wouldn't be surprised if the average life expectancy approached 85-90 years within 30-40 years.

Because we are living longer (or am I just going grey earlier?), we have to save more money to fund a longer retirement period. Social Security will soon be kaputnicksville. Company pensions aren't so big. The responsibility is on you to do the saving and investing. Like you didn't have enough on your plate with running a business! Right?

I'm in the trenches doing retirement planning with my clients. Here's what I'm seeing:

All of my clients play backgammon, do needlepoint, play bingo, and go to the 4 p.m. dinner buffets for $15. They all live in Florida and wear white leather shoes. (Still reading? See below for the real stuff.)

Many of my clients aren't retiring cold turkey. They are retiring later than they thought they would. As business owners, they are working part time. Why? Because they either need the money or because they love what they do.

They are considering selling part of their business but they are still working as a partial owner and receiving some cash flow. Cha-ching!

My clients are having mini-retirements. They work for a few years, take a year off, learn something new, and use the new skill to do something new. They're rock stars. They are having more fun while they work.

By doing some part-time work, my clients feel like they are more engaged in their lives. The thought of playing golf every day and eating bon bons just doesn't do it for them.

Working part-time in retirement could impact your investment portfolio.

If you work part-time or just retire later, there is more time for you to let your money compound (grow) and work for you. Word up.

If you are in your 30's or 40's, even your 50's, you may be able to take more risk in your portfolio because you won't need the money as soon as you think.

Your risk tolerance may not change, but your capacity to take risk may be bigger. Please note, I am not telling you to take more risk—everyone's financial situation is different.

If you start saving early enough, you may not have to save as much as you think. Major humungo caveat: most people haven't saved enough to fund their retirement, but working part-time in retirement sure does help.

Key takeaway: You have to plan to live as long as Yoda did. You don't want to run out of money. You need a plan. Pay yourself first in your biz and "May the Force be with you."

Looking for a simple plan? Check out my 5 wealth building strategies. Just go to the back of the book in the resources area.

Where Do All My Socks Go?

Why do I keep losing my socks?

What's up with that?

I suck at keeping my socks organized. I need a sock intervention.

I hope there is not a direct connection with my sock organization skills and my financial management skills.

Wanna get better at keeping track of your money? Especially the important financial stuff?

Here are 6 pieces of financial info that you should have at your fingertips incase of emergency or just in case you need to refer to them:

1. Your most recent tax return—for both personal and business
2. A copy of your living trust. Don't know what a living trust is? You may need one. Just Google "What is a living trust?"
3. All of your insurance stuff, including life insurance and business insurance policies. You need the policy numbers, the coverage amount of your insurance, and the names of the insurance companies.
4. The names, telephone numbers, and email addresses of your accountant, financial advisor, and estate attorney.

5. A quarterly profit-loss report for your business.
6. A recent statement of your investment, savings accounts, and bank accounts.

All of this can be stored on your local computer. You also may want to store this on a USB flash drive and keep it somewhere other than in your house.

I would also store it in a secure place online like: Dropbox, Hightail, or Carbonite.

Key takeaway: Chip away at these 6 items above. Do it over time. You'll feel more organized. And if you find any of my socks, send 'em my way.

Why Do So Many Guys Wear Their Pants Too Short?

I see it everywhere. In business meetings, in hotel lobbies, at the airport.

Tons of guys in suit pants that are one foot off the ground. Or their jeans are too short. I used to call them floods when I was a kid. These guys have no idea.

They need an intervention. Someone has to have a heart-to-heart with them.

This got me thinking. So many people aren't AWARE of what's going on with their finances. They've either made a decision just to not deal with their money, or whoever is advising them isn't keeping them abreast of what's going on with their finances.

Their money pants are too short.

Here are the top 9 things that you might not know about your finances:

1. **You may be invested in the wrong stuff** and you are really not diversified. I have referred to this stuff as asset classes—

the types of things you can invest in like stocks, bonds, cash, commodities, etc.

2. **You don't know what the 5 key drivers** are to increasing sales in your business.
3. **You are working with a financial advisor who is not a fiduciary.** That means he/she doesn't legally have to put your interests first.
4. **You are earning nothing,** zilch, no interest on the cash that you have in your checking, savings, or business account.
5. **You aren't getting properly serviced by your accountant.** That means he/she isn't calling you with tax planning ideas that may save you money. You deserve better service! After all, aren't you paying for it when you write a check to your CPA?
6. **You are eligible to open and invest in a Roth IRA.** When you retire, taxes will affect the amount of financial freedom you may have. Ask your financial advisor about this.
7. **You don't know what your monthly nut is.** You don't know how much money you spend every month. I'm talking both business money AND personal money.
8. **You are going to run out of money in retirement** and you are going to have to work longer than you thought.
9. **You don't have a bookkeeper.** You are doing your books by yourself.

It doesn't have to be this way. Next time you see a guy with short pants, you need to be the fashion police and set him straight. He has no idea how he looks.

Key takeaway: Get your head out of the sand. You need to know more about what's going on in your business. It's time to deal.

Financial Planning.
It's Not an F-Word—
Action Plan Part One

M ost of the time, your goals are going to cost money.
There are three ways you could fund your goals:

Make the same money and spend less

Make more money and spend the same

Make more money and spend less money

You have to choose which one you are going to do.

By making a choice, you are consciously deciding the path you are going to take. You are making a decision. And that's awesome.

So write down which number you choose and why.

One of your goals most likely will be retirement.

Here's what you need to know:

Where is the money going to come from?

An investment portfolio? The sale of your business? Working part-time? Real estate? Social Security? No way!

You need to have a general idea of where the money will come from.

The ONE THING that you need to be doing is building assets that will produce cash flow.

Enough cash flow to cover your living expenses.

Answer these two questions:

Where will the money come from when I retire?

Where am I going to put my money so that it can grow and produce income to fund my retirement?

Once you know these two answers, it's time to build out a financial plan for your retirement. Consider working with a fee-only financial advisor for customized advice. Many fee-only advisors can be found at www.napfa.org.

Financial Planning.
It's Not an F-Word—
Action Plan Part Two

There's no such thing as a self-made millionaire. Everyone gets help. You can't succeed by doing everything on your own.

My grandma used to tell me, "Justin, you can't see the hump on your own back."

Whether it's your business or personal money, you need an outsider's perspective.

You need customized advice that is tailored to your own unique financial situation.

That means you need to get a little vulnerable. And show your financial stuff to someone. A professional "someone."

They are there to help you, with no judgment.

Here's a short list of professional service providers you want on your team:

- Accountant
- Bookkeeper

- Financial Advisor/Financial Planner
- Business coach
- Marketing expert
- Attorney
- Personal banker
- Insurance broker

You might not think you need all of these people, but lemme tell ya, if you want to take your business to the next level, you will eventually need all of them.

You don't have to go out and hire all of these people right away.

But I want you to build relationships with them now. You never know when you might need one of them.

Put a checkmark next to the numbers above where you have an existing relationship with someone you like. Go out and form relationships with the service providers that are not circled.

Talk to them on the phone. Take meetings.

Don't worry about making a list of questions to ask them.

It's all about the questions they ask you. If they start out talking about how great they are, how many years they have been in business, how much money they make—they are not for you.

Do you feel that they really care about you? What kinds of questions are they asking you? Are they actively listening to you?

It's all about you. Not about them. They need to get to know you.

That way, they can point out the humps on your back.

$

Financial Planning.
It's Not an F-Word—
Action Plan Part Three

I t is really important to understand the numbers in your business. You need clarity. No more flying by the seat of your pants. It's time to know your numbers.

It's so much easier to have someone just tell you these numbers rather than you having to figure them out on your own.

That someone is your bookkeeper.

If you are doing your own books, in most cases, your time is better spent on revenue generating activities.

It's time to be proactive. Not reactive.

Tell your bookkeeper you want them to tell you the following every month:

1. Sales
2. Expenses
3. Profits

4. The two biggest things that happened in your business that affected the cash
5. Who you owe money to
6. Who owes money to you

Numbers 1-3 can be found on your profit-loss statement.

Number 4 can be found on your statement of cash flows.

Numbers 5 and 6 can be found on your balance sheet.

Have your bookkeeper email this stuff to you by the 10th of every month, for the prior month.

Once you get this info from your bookkeeper, I want you to input it into this cash flow PDF tool I created.

Just go to the back of the book to see where you can download it.

It will help you manage your cash flow and make you feel like you're in control.

It's simple to use.

Your Business: A Game Changer for Your Money—Introduction

I f you don't know what you're going to do with the money you make, you'll never be motivated to go out and make it.

So what is it that you want?

What do you *really* want? And how much does it cost?

I want you to use your business as the engine to drive your wealth. Your business must serve your life. Your life doesn't have to serve your business.

Enjoy this section. I enjoyed writing this stuff for you!

Just go out and take some action.

"Twenty years from now you will be more disappointed by the things that you didn't do than by the ones that you did do. So throw off the bowlines. Sail away from the safe harbor. Catch the trade winds in your sails. Explore. Dream. Discover."

—Mark Twain

2 Years from Now

The year is almost over. How'd your biz do? I hope you crushed it. In 2 years—that's right, 2 years—I want you to have a year like you have never imagined.

Here's the dealio. If you make next year the year of marketing, you could have a killer year in 2 years!

Marketing takes time—usually 12 to 18 months for a campaign to really kick in and give you results. This year, and even next year, I'd like you to double the amount of money you spend on marketing.

Did I just say spend? Ugh! I meant invest. Why invest? Because the money has got to come back—like some boomerang sha-bang!

Last year I looked at a bunch of profit-loss statements from small businesses. Exciting right?

They were spending 2-5% on marketing. That's not enough! Double down. You don't even have to go to Vegas. Try investing between 5-10% of your business revenue on marketing. Get serious. Get wild. I am challenging you to do that right here. If you don't, then you will get the same results for the next two years.

When you invest in your business through marketing, you need to think about the return on your investment. The sooner you make money from implementing your marketing plan, the less risky it will be to double your marketing budget. That's because you are getting paid sooner, which is so key when you are doubling down.

No more investing, hoping that the cash will come back. That money has gotta come back, especially if you are just starting a biz.

If you don't have the extra money to increase your marketing budget, then you have no choice but to double the amount of time you spend on marketing.

How?

Start delegating nonessential tasks to others.

Make sure you continue to serve your clients and customers well.

Yes, it's a little bit of a juggling act, but if you have the time management thing down, you can double down. Time or money. You pick.

Imagine what things could be like in 2 years. Tons of people want to do business with you. Or your products are selling like hotcakes. Think about how cool it would be to have your business results fund your personal goals.

Maybe you just want to have more money in the bank.

Maybe you want more financial independence.

Maybe you just want to go to Nordstrom without worrying about how much those boots cost!

Maybe you want to travel more and see the world.

How about being debt free?

How about buying that dream home of yours?

I believe in your 2-year plan. I'm with you. I'm doubling down too.

Key takeaway: A well-executed marketing campaign could take 12-18 months to really work. Think of a 2-year plan and double your investment in marketing.

I Know I Don't Know

If you don't know what you don't know and you screw up, it's not the end of the world. Why? Because you had no idea what you were doing in the first place!

The key is to be more aware of what you are doing. Get smart. Read. Learn from others. Become more informed.

Maybe you should hang out with Alex Trebek, host of the TV show Jeopardy! He has all the answers, but has he made all of the mistakes? That guy thinks he is such a stud. Whatever.

I bet Alex Trebek doesn't know this:

"4 Mistakes That Entrepreneurs Make When They Plan Their Retirement."

1. **You plan to sell your business in the year you want to retire.** Then you will take that money and live off it. But what happens if you sell your business for less than the amount you think you can get for it? You may have to work longer than you'd like, or you may have to reduce your lifestyle in retirement.

   Consider the following factors that may increase the value of your business:

The quality of your client base.

The quality of the systems that you have in your business.

The degree to which your business relies on you—the key person—and what your unique competitive advantage is.

Even though you could be years away from selling, the sooner you improve these attributes, the earlier your business could gain enterprise value.

2. **All your eggs are in one basket—your business.** It's important to diversify your net worth. Consider saving 10-15% of your income into some type of retirement plan. You won't have all your chips on the table and you'll be able to take advantage of great profitable years in your business by taking part of that income and stocking it away for a rainy day.

3. **Taxes.** Use an after-tax figure when estimating what you will net when you sell your business. Ask your CPA if the sale will be taxed at a long-term capital gains rate vs. your ordinary income tax rate. Also, set money aside each quarter to pay your estimated taxes or the taxes that will be due each year. That way, you won't be stuck with a huge tax bill at the end of the year. That's the worst!

4. **Limited time set aside to plan for what you want.** You are consumed by your business. Think about what your life in retirement will look like.

Where do you want to retire to?

What do you want to retire from?

What does your perfect week look like in retirement?

What are you doing?

Who are you doing it with?

Get into a nice conversation with yourself! Think about this stuff. These answers will make it easier for you to come up with what your expenses in retirement could be.

Key takeaway: Planning for retirement is a process. Chip away at it. You'll begin to have clarity. That way, the decisions you make along your life journey will bring you closer to what you want later on in life—and maybe even today. Yep. That sounds right.

6 Things to Learn
from Jimmy Buffett

1. **He has a great team of trusted advisors.** His advisors work together on behalf of Jimbo. It's a coordinated approach all centered around his needs. Jimmy is the main guy. Also, everyone knows everyone. They are in constant communicado.
2. **He's a smart businessman.** He reads, likes to learn, and has made a decision to get educated. He gets the fact that it's easier to make financial decisions when he really understands what his options are with his money.
3. **The guy has like 5 different sources of revenue,** all built around his core brand—feeling good and living life. How cool is that?
4. **He gets out of his office.** He tours. He connects with his clients and he gives them what they want: good music and an amazing experience.
5. **He believes in taking risks.** I would call them calculated risks. It all starts with leveraging his brand, trying new things, being open to failure, and just giving to his peeps. This message is in his lyrics and you can see it in the actions he takes as an entrepreneur.

6. **He's a philanthropist.** He is such a giver. He's all about the environment. He is down to earth. Jimmy's fans feel like they are part of a Jimmy Buffett movement.

Key takeaway: You have to be a business rock star. Go out and meet new people. It's time to have fun. It's time to make money. It's time to elevate your brand. Let's go!

$29 Salad?

I t's a beautiful day. You want to be outside. You've been holed up in your office all week.

So you go to a fancy-schmancy hotel for lunch.

It's on the beach. Gorgeous view. The ocean is amazing. The water is so blue. The sun is shining on the blue ocean. Very romantic. The whole deal.

Montage Laguna Beach anyone?

You and your date go. You order 2 chopped salads and get 2 waters. You really don't look at the prices on the menu.

It was a lovely lunch, until you get the bill—for $65!

What? 29 bucks for a salad?

Yep.

What if the salad was $10 and they charged you $19 for the view?

Or you brought your own salad and just asked to pay for the $19 view?

Or if you ordered the salad and got a deal because you turned around with your back to the ocean and didn't have to pay for the view!

Ha!

It doesn't work that way.

If you plan on eating, you have to pay for the view and pay for the food! That's the only way it's priced.

Of course you could sit on a nearby bench or just take a walk around the hotel, but if you want to have a bite or a drink, you're paying full boat, baby. $29.

They are not giving you the choice to buy just the salad or just the view.

If people just bought the salad or the view, the hotel wouldn't make enough money to cover their costs and make a profit.

You can't give your customers an option to buy something if you lose money. If you do, you better have an up-sell where you make money.

It's perfectly fine to give your customers a choice when they buy stuff. But at each price point, you must cover your costs and make a profit.

Don't undervalue yourself. It's not just about the product you are selling. It's the result or outcome. That's the view at the hotel . . . it's what people are paying for.

Key takeaway: You must price your products and services to make money—wait—to make a PROFIT. Otherwise, you will run out of money.

What Your Peers Do in the A.M.

B edhead. Terrible breath. Hitting snooze. Staying in bed. Coffee. Checking Facebook for an hour.

We all have our morning routine. We all have the same 24 hours in a day.

Secret: the most successful entrepreneurs rock at managing their time, especially the first 3 hours in their day. These 3 hours are GOLD to them. It's when they get shiz done.

I have interviewed a bunch of people, done some research, and have compiled a list of 6 things that successful entrepreneurs do in the morning before 10 a.m. Hopefully you can integrate a few of these into your morning and get more done in less time.

How cool is that?

Eat a solid breakfast. Get some protein in you. Get your brain in high performance mode. You know this, right? But are you doing it?

Exercise or stretch. Get the blood flowing. Go for a run. Take a swim. Go to the gym. Go on a brisk walk. Do something.

Make a list of what you need to do for the day. Rank them in order of importance. No matter what else happens, make completing those tasks a priority.

Completing the most important task(s) of the day was the most frequent answer I got. Some people focus on their creative work first. They see themselves as more creative earlier in the day.

Many don't check social media in the first 2 hours of the a.m., unless their biz heavily relies on it.

Don't check email first thing (like within 30 minutes of waking up) in the morning. Checking email means that you are focusing on other people's priorities rather than your own. Sending emails is different because you are initiating something that you want to get done. Strategy, baby!

Start with one hour dedicated to you. Listen to inspiring music. Meditate, exercise, stretch.

Wake up early. Almost everyone gave me this answer. Many entrepreneurs feel more productive in the morning. They get up before anyone else in the house does. They cherish that quiet time. And they DO stuff.

Key takeaway: The first few hours of the day belong to you. Be smart with your time.

Bad Gas at Macy's

My wife and I had to buy our shma-geggy (crazy) kids some nice clothes for a Bar Mitzvah this weekend, so we decided to go to the mall and hit up a few department stores.

First stop: Macy's. What a disaster that place was. It wasn't well lit. I shoulda brought a flashlight.

There were clothes and racks everywhere. It was a total obstacle course. The Macy's presentation was a hodgepodge. It looked like my garage. Mondo bizarro.

Plus, there was no one really there on the floor to help us. It was like someone had bad gas and just cleared everyone out!

We were done. Gonzo. In about 3 minutes, we just bailed.

We worked our way over to Nordstrom. *Way* nicer. Well lit, the clothes were neatly hung on the racks. It wasn't schlocky (trashy, cheap) at all.

There was more space to look around and there were actually people there to help us. Partay!

Nordstrom got me. Within 10 seconds, I was subconsciously ready to buy and I hadn't even made it up to the kids' section yet!

It was all in the presentation. I felt more at ease inside the store. They had great music playing. I was singin' along in my head, rockin' my stuff.

Someone from Nordstrom came up to help me right away. She asked me what I was looking for, gave me some options, and boom! In 5 minutes, I was done.

It was easy-peezy lemon-squeezy and I felt good about my purchase.

For me, it was all about the experience, the buying experience.

This made me rethink what my clients' and customers' experiences are. I want to up-level my stuff and make my peeps feel even more amazing about their experiences.

I want them to feel at home. I want them to get jiggy with it. I'm talking easy like Sunday morning. Lionel style. Krane style.

So whatchu got? How are you making your buyers and prospects feel? What kind of experiences are you giving them?

Consider taking some of these steps:

1. **Spy on your competition.** Go out and buy your competition's stuff. Seriously, do it this weekend. Go through the whole experience. Think about what you could do to make your clients' experiences better. Your stuff must be different.

2. **Wow your peeps.** Go over the top with a total "OMG" factor. Then they will tell their friends. Seth Godin talks about this all the time. If you can't create your way out of a paper bag like me, go hire some people to KraneStorm with you.

3. **Make a financial investment in your business.** Make your peeps feel like milk chocolate. Do you even know how much money you are investing in this particular area? My guess is, very little. Step up. Make it happen. Giddy-up!

Key takeaway: Your packaging and presentation DO make a difference. They help people buy your stuff. So why not invest in this and do it right?

Business Pooh-Pooh Model

B usiness model, schmiz-ness model. I used to pooh-pooh this term until I started studying how successful entrepreneurs think and really strategize their businesses.

Your business model is basically how your business makes money. For example, how you attract prospects, convert them into clients, and make a profit. Ya know, the good stuff.

If you are in a service-based business, the most common way to work with clients is on a one-on-one basis. This has its advantages and disadvantages. The upside of the one-on-one model is that someone is paying you for your help. It's a great feeling when you see the results that your clients get from taking your advice. It's like seeing your kids win a gold medal.

And it becomes even better when your clients are paying you what you are worth, right? Subliminal message: raise your prices.

You ever pee in your pants?

What happens when you have a full plate of clients and you are crazy busy? Like when you can't even get away from your desk to go to the bathroom? You don't have time to review your profit-loss statement, get a massage, or even take a vacation. Bummer.

If you have a full plate when it comes to clients, I'll bet you wish you didn't have to work so hard to make about the same amount of money year in and year out.

A better business model is to have scale, leverage, and passive income, in addition to working one-on-one with clients. Can we go to the moon already?!

Leveraged income is when you work with multiple clients at one time. It's not one-to-one. It's one to many.

Here's an example of how leveraged income works:

Let's say you're a nutritionist and your hourly rate is $100. If you spent the same hour teaching a one-hour class with ten people paying $30, you just tripled your money to $300. You're spending the same amount of time, but you're bringing in more money.

Here's an example of how passive income works:

Passive income is when you don't have to be actively involved in doing the work to get paid. Let's say you are an accountant. You are still looking for clients but you want to make money while you are on vacation, so you decide to create a workbook for people to use for their taxes.

Your upfront costs are $2,000. This is the time it took you to write it, design it, and get it up for sale on your website. You sell it for $50. When people buy the workbook on your site, you don't have to do anything. It automatically gets shipped and you get paid.

You are drinking Mai Tais in Hawaii while people buy your product. Sweetness.

If you don't have enough clients, you need to build scalable and leveraged programs/services/products/offerings **at the same time you are building up your one-on-one business. This is so huge! OMG, I wish I had known this when I started in business.**

So how do you do this?

Write down all of your services and package them into a few programs. Price the one-on-one service to be more expensive.

Create a passive or leveraged product and price it lower to attract more people who may want to test the waters with a less expensive product, but make sure you are pricing it to make a profit, not break even.

Create a line item for marketing the items in your new business model. Consider investing at least 5% of your business revenue on marketing. Why? Because if you don't, how will anyone know about your programs or want to buy them?

In these new leveraged and passive programs, create them in a way that you get paid over a longer period of time and not just once. Recurring income is super important.

Key takeaway: As you build your empire, remember that it's OK to work one-on-one, but make sure your business also has leveraged or passive income components to it. It's a much better business model, and I'll bet you will be happier with the results.

Not everyone is going to be your cheerleader, especially when you're doing something different to grow your business. You need support. Accountability. Join a mastermind.

Can You Get Things Done at the Office?

E ver go to a restaurant with your significant other for a nice romantic meal, but it doesn't quite turn out that way?

You look at the menu, you're trying to find something to order, and then you hear this really loud voice from one table over.

You start to eavesdrop. You're trying not to, but the guy's voice at the other table is *so* freakin' loud. This guy is a total talker. He is going on and on about nothing and doesn't stop for the entire meal. So annoying! You can't even concentrate and find something to order!

What a doozy.

Concentration and focus is huge in business too.

Do you ever feel like you need to get away from the office to get work done? Your employees sometimes distract you. The phone never stops ringing (I know, that's a good thing), or it's just too hard for you not to check email.

Ever feel like you're in reactive mode rather than proactive mode?

In business, sometimes you need to get away and be by yourself. You need some peace and quiet. Yes, you need days off to rejuvenate, but this time, I'm talking about taking time away from the office to strategize.

I believe you are supposed to break free of your current plateau in your biz.

Want a game changer? You need to block time and I'm not talking 2 or 3 hours, I'm talking days. (You can even start with just 1 day.) Take yourself off the grid. Go AWOL. No email, no phone calls, no Facebook, nothing. It's time for you to just do your strategy and then implement all the cool stuff you want to do.

Some of this time you may need to share with your team. During this time, you need to make sure that you have enough support to service your clients and customers while you're off the grid.

In the beginning, blocking days is going to be challenging. The question is, how are you going to show up and meet this challenge?

Do it. Take your business to the next level. Do it to make more money. Do it so the money can pay for your personal goals.

Here's my list of strategic things you can do on your block-out-time days:

1. **Identify new promotional partners** to align yourself with. Reach out to them.
2. **Create an operations manual.** Not sure how to do it? Just start adding processes and procedures. Just little things that you repeatedly do all the time. Do the same for your employees. It's all about creating systems. It's a way to be more productive.
3. **Create a tax plan.** Call your CPA to create a plan to pay taxes throughout the year so you don't get a tax surprise in April.
4. **Assess your pricing and product choices.** Do you need to revise your pricing? Are you giving your peeps enough choices to buy from? Do you have a premium product/service offering?
5. **Leverage technology.** Do this to automate more things in your business. Upgrade your computers, get better software, Google

"CRM software" and see what software you can use to be more productive.

6. **Write 5 blog posts for the next 5 weeks.**
7. **List 4 things you can farm out to people on elance.com.** Then farm them out.

    This is huge for me.
8. **Do some market research.** Create a survey to learn something new that will result in more biz. Listen to your customers to see what else you can offer them.
9. **Read an entire business book** that you just haven't had the time to read.
10. **Create a social media plan for your business.**

Start your block-out-time days with meditation, a walk, protein, and all of that good stuff. Let yourself think rather than just react. Let your ideas and thoughts come to you. You will have more clarity on what you should be doing.

Key takeaway: Go someplace different to work on your strategic stuff. Use these days to reconnect to what is meaningful for you—all of those business projects that you wish you had the time for. Enjoy the journey. You'll feel great.

I'm All Choked Up

I'm getting a little fahklempt—SO choked up!
Why?

If you have kids and you see them having loads of fun, you get crazy happy.

What were they up to? The good ol' trampoline, but this thing is gigunda.

It's got a basketball hoop inside of it.

They are on that thing every time they go to my parents' house.

My son dunks a basketball and my daughter does some serious cartwheels in there.

Once they go in, they stay in forever. Why? Because it makes them feel good. They never get bored with it.

That trampoline makes them feel like they have super jumping powers. What kid doesn't like the feeling of jumping up to the sky?

That got me thinking, I deal with ROI (return on your investment) all of the time when I work with entrepreneurs. It's always good to shoot for the best bang for your buck.

So . . .

What is the least amount of money you can spend in your business that can make your buyers feel like they are a kid on a trampoline? That's the type of ROI I'm talking about.

You're a business owner. You want more clients and more sales. You want to make more moolah. You know you need to differentiate yourself. You want an edge, so you create a marketing plan, or you launch a referral campaign, or you do a joint venture with someone who serves the same market you do. This is all good stuff.

But you're missing one key thing: feeling fahklempt (Yiddish for "choked up with emotion"). Excuse me while I grab a tissue because it truly is all about the feelings.

The way you make your clients feel is what makes your biz go en fuego. You want your customers to feel the wow when they buy from you. If your customers feel amazing, they will keep buying from you. They are going to tell their friends, and then it goes on Facebook, and the key influencers get excited, and on and on.

Think about this for a sec: it always comes back to the feelings. How are you making your customers feel? I am challenging you right here to think strategically about what you can do to wow the heck out of your tribe of buyers.

Do stuff that they aren't expecting at all. Do the stuff that no one else is doing. Spy on your competition. What are they up to? Same old same old, right?

So, what are you up to? I hope your answer isn't a whole lot of nothing. Let's get original. Crazy. Wild. Different. Distinct. Cool. Wow.

Like jumping to the sky on a trampoline.

Key takeaway: Make your customers feel amazing when they buy your stuff *and* when they use/consume your stuff.

Did You Ding-Dong Ditch Me?

There is a knock at your door. You open the door and no one is there. You heard someone knocking . . . surprise! You have been ding-dong ditched by your retirement plan.

You know it's going to happen again because at some point, retirement will be staring at you in the face and you will have to pay for it. Oy vey.

Your business is an asset and you should start thinking about how you can monetize it to partially fund your retirement.

Priming your business to be sold successfully before you retire is like falling into a boatload of cash with a lot of perks.

It would allow you to spend more money now and not have to save as much for retirement.

You also would not have to take as much risk with your investments to fund your retirement. So instead of relying on an aggressive portfolio made up mostly of stock funds, you could invest in a potentially more moderate risk portfolio of a mix of stocks and bonds. You would probably take less risk, and it might be a smoother investing ride. But remember, there are no guarantees that you will definitely take less risk.

Retirement planning is all about cash flow planning. How much money will you need every month in retirement and what will the sources be? One obvious example of a cash flow source in retirement is Social Security.

But c'mon, how long will Social Security be around and how much will you really get? If you are under 40 years old—fuhgeddaboutit! Nada. Zilch. Le Goose Egg. Zero.

Many people think that their spending will go down during retirement, but during the first 5 years, it may actually go up!

That's because you are going to be a rock star. You will have more free time. You may travel more, go out to dinner more, and do things that you didn't have a chance to do while you were working. That all adds up to spending more money.

Bottom line? Get some cash flow from the sale of your business. You won't be ding-dong ditched from your retirement plan.

Whether you sell services or tangible products, you need to lay the groundwork to make your business attractive and appealing to potential buyers. An entrepreneur with tangible products may have an easier time selling the company.

But what if you are a business owner who provides services?

How much is your business worth if you are no longer there?

You will need to set up a succession plan to transfer your clients to someone else. One easy way to do this is to bring the buyer in while you still own the business. You teach them how to do what you do and allow them to build relationships with your clients while you are still there.

How cool is that?

This lets your clients get to know your buyer, rather than just handing them off the day you retire.

This scenario also can allow the buyer to buy your company over time, which may be more affordable and attractive for a potential buyer.

Basically, you need to see your succession plan as a process and not simply as a transaction, and it will need to accomplish two things:

Gradually transfer client relationships from you to another person or group of people.

A gradual transfer of all your management responsibilities.

Don't ditch your retirement plan. I want you to have a killer lifestyle down the road.

Key takeaway: Make your business sellable. That way, you could walk away with a fat pile of cash. You could fly away on your magic carpet into the sunset.

Did Your Raisinets Get Stuck?

It happens to everyone. It's like a rite of passage. You go to the vending machine to buy your Raisinets (major chocolate fix, right?). You put your money in the machine and your food gets stuck.

You're bummed out.

You weren't expecting this to happen. You're faced with the decision of putting more money in the machine to get what you want or calling some number to complain (do they ever answer?), knowing you will never get your money back.

Doesn't it stink when you spend money and you don't get what you paid for? Or you have to pony up more money when you thought you wouldn't have to? Especially if it's for your business?

First off, when you spend money in your business, think of it as an investment. Don't just think of it as an expense. That way, you will be in the mindset of getting a return on your money, which is really what you are paying for.

Let's pretend you are considering hiring a marketing consultant to redo your whole brand. Here are 5 things you need to ask yourself, so your Raisinets don't get stuck:

1. **Is the fee a one-time fee or will you pay as you go?** How much time does the fee cover? One week, six months, twenty years (you still reading this?), or as long as it takes to get what you want? It's important to be really clear about the length of the engagement. That way, there will be no surprises.

2. **Does the fee cover advice and implementation?** Sometimes you will get advice to do something, and then you will have to go implement the advice and pay again. For example, your marketing person may advise you to create a company brochure. But what if the fee didn't include the cost to literally create it? You'd have to pay again. Total stinker. You wouldn't even get your Raisinets.

3. **What's the price for each round of editing?** Most marketing plans include 2 or 3 rounds of edits. Find out the pricing for each additional round (the 3rd or 4th). Use your edits wisely, so you don't have to spend extra money. Get those Raisinets the first time!

4. **Am I getting adequate communication updates?** So many marketing people are highly creative and have amazing ideas. But sometimes they fall off the face of the earth (like your contractor) and they are nowhere to be found. Make sure your marketing person gives you weekly status updates, so you can track your progress. It's the worst feeling in the world to pay for marketing and get no status updates! Jeez. Try paying as you go for marketing help. That way, the marketing person has skin in the game and will need to show up to get paid.

5. **What's the scope of the project?** You need to be clear on what you are specifically paying for. For example, if you are paying for a website design and a logo, that is all you will receive. If it turns out that you also need a Facebook business page, then that will be more money. Just make a list of what you are paying for, so you can get what you pay for and stay on track. Wait a minute—don't make a list! Ask your marketing person to give you a proposal and an outline of what you will get.

There you have it. No more marketing money getting stuck in the vending machine. It's time for you to get your Raisinets.

Key takeaway: When you hire marketing consultants to do work for you, make sure you get what you pay for and that the agreement/contract is super clear.

Do Your Kids Forget?

What is it with these kids? Ever put your kids to bed and realize that they didn't brush their teeth? Or that they didn't remember to pick up their toys? Or they didn't remember to wash behind their ears!

OMG! What is going on here? They forget. They're on to the next thing.

Makes me think of all the steps and things we need to remember to do as entrepreneurs to bring in more business and better service our existing clients.

The more that you are on top of the important things you need to get done, the more money you will probably end up making in your business.

So what can you do to make sure things don't fall through the cracks?

Write a systems manual. List out all of the steps that need to be taken as you service your clients. Do you have to do every step? Can any of them be delegated to someone who works with you?

Leverage your client database management software. Set up a simple task like notifying you when your clients' birthdays are. Google "CRM database management." There are tons of companies like SalesForce that can help you automate your client management system.

Use Google Voice. Instead of sending emails to yourself or your assistant as a reminder, set up a Google phone number. Now you can make use of your time while you're in your car. You can then call into your Google Voice number and leave a message. Google then converts your message into text and the words can be sent via email.

Leverage your vendors. You are giving them business every month. Is there anything they could do for you on a consistent basis? Here's an example: let's say you want to do a client mailer campaign. Instead of using your printer to just print and mail your stationery, use him to do a mailer and actually send it out for you. And ask for a deal since he's now getting some new business from you.

Key takeaway: Set up systems in your business. No more forgetting. That way, you can be more productive in your biz.

Do Your Taxes Have Bad Breath?

E ver get into a conversation with someone who has terrible breath? You are trying to back away from them, but their stank is just ra-dic?

They have no idea how bad their breath is! Especially after they eat that onion bagel with lox cream cheese! You'll do anything to avoid their halitosis.

Got me thinking, do your taxes have bad breath?

Your taxes only end up stinking if you put them off 'til the last minute. It stinks to have no idea how much money you owe the IRS.

Give your taxes a breath mint! No more scrambling the last few days before taxes are due. No more tax surprises. No more bad breath.

How you plan your taxes is most likely how you plan your financial life. Be proactive, not reactive, my dah-ling.

Here's my step-by-step plan on how to stay on top of your taxes.

1. **Keep your books/financial records current.** Hire a bookkeeper. You didn't get into business to enter all of your receipts/bills into QuickBooks by yourself. This should not be your day job. No more 10 p.m. data entry after your kids go to bed. Why not watch *Homeland* instead?

2. **Speak with your accountant every quarter** (better than getting a root canal, right?). Give them your quarterly profit-loss statement. Review it with them. Ask your CPA to tell you what you owe in taxes for that quarter. Then when you get the amount owed, pay the taxes then. Don't wait 'til the end of the year. You will forget.

   You might spend your tax money somewhere else and then it's game over. If you do this every quarter, you will most likely have paid enough in taxes and you won't get hit with a huge bill.

3. **Ask your CPA how you are going to pay your taxes.** Will it be through withholding from a salary, or just based on paying estimated taxes?

4. **Make sure you have the correct entity for your business.** Should you be a sole proprietor, LLC, or an S Corp? Ask your CPA if you need to take a salary to pay your taxes. Most of the time, S Corps and C Corps have to pay salaries to you.

5. **Report sizeable realized gains to your CPA.** A realized gain is when you buy something (stocks/mutual funds, etc.) and sell it for a profit, in a taxable account.

Why do all of this tax planning stuff?

Because now we can have a clearer idea of how much money we have left. Our money is dying to talk with us!

Key takeaway: It's so much easier to have a conversation with your money when you know how much money is yours, not the IRS's. Give your taxes a breath mint. Tax planning isn't that bad after all. It sets you up for doing what you want with your money.

Extra Credit for Your Biz

We gotta dive into giving you some credit! Yep. Business credit. Ways you can borrow money for your business. And I'm not talking about personal credit cards.

I'm talkin' business credit cards or lines of credit, people! These lines of credit can be issued by banks or even by your suppliers. Sometimes when your business borrows money, the bank or credit card companies won't make you sign a personal guarantee. That means if your business goes under, the creditors can't come after your personal money.

Do you know that you can have a business credit score? Just like a personal FICO score? Yeah, that's right! Your business credit score ranges from 0-100. The higher the score, the better.

Your business credit score depends on if you pay your company bills on time, what your business cash flow is, etc. Remember, your score is primarily based on your company's financial numbers. Your personal credit score is a smaller factor in determining your business credit score.

So why should you establish business credit anyway?

Having business credit diversifies your borrowing options and sometimes your liability. If you use your personal credit to finance your business and your business goes under, your personal credit will be affected. Your FICO score will go down.

Total stinker.

Having business credit is pretty cool. It separates your personal credit from your business credit. You can actually build business credit even if your personal credit stinks.

The higher the business credit score you have, the more money you may be able to borrow from a bank, and the lower the interest rate could be. Some businesses can borrow more money using business credit rather than personal credit.

Here's what you can do right now. It's easy like a Sunday morning, like baking a cake. Just follow these steps:

1. **Your business needs to be an entity.** It can't be a sole proprietorship. In order to get business credit, you need to have an LLC or a corporation. Review with your attorney or accountant.
2. **Get a federal tax ID number for your business.** Your accountant or attorney can do this for you.
3. **Set up a bank account in your business name.**
4. **Get a business credit card.**
5. **Make sure your business licenses and state/federal tax returns are all filed.**
6. **Get your company listed on the 411.com and yellowpages. com directories.**
7. **Check out the Dun & Bradstreet website** and consider getting a D-U-N-S number. The number is available to the public, which could increase your company's image. Go to: www.dandb.com/ establish-business-credit/
8. **Call your suppliers** and see if they will give you a line of credit or a business credit card. When you buy from them on a regular basis and pay them off, they notify the credit agencies.

Key takeaway: Get business credit. It could help you.

Get Paid

Schnitzeling: the act of moving money around from account to account. A little here, a little there.

You're schnitzeling. Baron Von Schnitzel. The Schnitzel-Meister. The Schnitzel-ator.

You take money out of your business whenever you need it. A little here, a little there. You love this system. Just get money whenever you need it. It's just like an ATM until you run into cash flow problems. Stay with me here.

If you willy-nilly it and take money from your business whenever you want to, there could be times in the month where you don't have enough money to pay yourself.

Bummer.

Game changer.

We've got to get you paid. Like first. Like. Right. Now. Let's get you in the habit of paying yourself first. I'm talking a regular consistent salary or draw. It needs to be high enough to meet your living expenses.

That way, you can cover your personal monthly nut, including Thursday night sushi.

In the back of your mind you're going to work smarter to make sure you have enough money to meet your new fixed salary.

Step 1: What's your personal monthly nut? If you know this, you can determine how much to pay yourself.

Step 2: Have a glass of Rosso Di Montalcino. Do whatever you need to do to get in a state of mind where your financial sitch isn't going to overwhelm you. That could be a little vino or a financial planner, CPA, or bookkeeper too.

Step 3: You need to know if you should pay yourself a salary, a draw, or a combination of both. A salary is where taxes are taken out of your paycheck. A draw is where you just take money and pay no taxes.

FYI, when you pay yourself a salary, here are the taxes that usually get taken out:

1. Social Security taxes
2. Medicare taxes
3. Federal taxes
4. State taxes
5. State disability payments

Stay with me. You really need to know this stuff so you won't have to worry so much about money. Keep drinking the Rosso.

Paying yourself a salary depends on what type of legal structure your business is. If you are a sole proprietor or single member LLC, you just take draws. If you take a draw, you must set aside enough money to pay your taxes. Work with your CPA on this.

If you are an S Corp, you must take a salary. You can take a draw as well. Many business owners take a low salary and take higher draws. They try to get around paying payroll (Social Security and Medicare) taxes. It's all fine and dandy, until the IRS audits you and they nail you.

It's generally recommended to pay yourself a minimum salary of 30-50% of your profits. You need to review these options with your accountant. Yes, that means you have to call them or just forward this to them. If they don't call you back and want to work on this with you, find someone who will.

Read this if you think you might need to raise/borrow money or sell your business: You're going to want to show the bank or your buyer that you consistently pay yourself a salary/draw. It just looks good.

Key takeaway: Pay yourself first, every month from your business. It's a nice little plan for yourself. Financial clarity is HUGE. Get my free cash flow calculator. It's simple to use and will help you take control of your money. Go to the back of the book in the resources tab for the deets.

He Wanted My Thin Mints

Man are those Thin Mints good. I will gladly pay $4 a box. Gimme 10 of them.

Pronto.

I put them in my freezer and have them for dessert. Ah-may-zing!

So this guy calls me up. He wants my Thin Mints. He wants to hire me as his financial planner.

He immediately asks me what I charge for my Thin Mints (my fees).

He probably wants to buy my Thin Mints for $3.50!

I was right. Keep reading . . .

Oh jeez.

Ding. Ding. Ding. The bell goes off in my head. This guy is shopping. He is price sensitive. Not who I want to deal with.

This guy was in poverty thinking mode. I could hear it in his voice. He was so concerned about how much it was going to cost.

He forgot about the benefit.

He wasn't thinking about what could be possible if he hired me—a better financial life.

So I asked him what he did for a living. He said he was a tutor and a consultant. I then asked him, what happens when his prospects call him and ask him about his fees right away.

He got the point that, usually, when someone asks you what your fees are in the first 15 seconds, they are major price sensitive. The relationship usually just doesn't work out.

I turned him down 30 seconds into the call. He was shocked. He couldn't believe I turned him down so quickly. I totally caught him off guard. He was expecting a nice discount.

He quickly got the point that I wasn't needy, that I was willing to walk away from a potential client.

You need to be this way with your prospects. It's time to stand up for yourself.

It's time to charge what you're worth. If you are getting enough at bats (meaning, chances to get business), then there is plenty of business to go around.

If you aren't getting enough business, then you need to be doing major marketing or change your marketing.

When people grind you on your fees, it's usually not their only expectation.

They start asking you to do other things like walk their dog, do some dry cleaning, and cook dinner! All the stuff that is outside the scope of what you do.

These people become toxic. You just need to cut them out. There are plenty of people who will pay your price.

Key takeaway: Charge what you're worth. Why? Because you are amazing at what you do. You're the best. For reelz. It's about personal dignity, baby.

Hello, Newman. Hello, Jerry.

S einfeld and Newman. Total rivals. Always scheming against one another.

But somehow, they managed to survive living on the same floor. A few times they even did things together and got along. Who woulda thunk?

Seinfeld and Newman are like Netflix and Comcast. Two competitors that are usually trying to "one up" one another.

But maybe not . . .

The *Wall Street Journal* reported that Netflix is in talks with Comcast to make its app (its content) available on Comcast's set top boxes. This deal would allow Netflix's online videos to be streamed through Comcast set top boxes.

The thinking is that both Comcast and Netflix could do some sort of rev share and both financially benefit.

Netflix. Comcast. You can learn a few things from this:

Having content and a platform for your content is *so* huge. Gigunda huge. You could have a killer blog, but if no one knows about it, and you don't have any distribution (in this case, a platform or a following), it's going to be pretty tough to grow your brand. That's why Netflix is approaching Comcast. Comcast has over 50 million subscribers. Netflix wants more distribution for its content.

If you want to make a giant leap, you can onesie-twosie things in your business for only so long. Consider strategic alliances that can give you scalability and leverage. Big time.

Consider a joint venture with your competition. Yep. Sandra Yancey, the CEO of eWomen Network, doesn't even use the word competition. She's all about co-opetition. Sandra defines it as collaborating and working together where both businesses benefit. Think differently. 1 plus 1 could equal 3.

Change with the times. There is a risk that Netflix could lose a bunch of customers if the studios decide to sell content direct to consumers, but by aligning with Comcast, they get more critical mass. Think of something that you know you need to do but haven't gotten around to doing to stay current in business. Mine is Google Hangouts.

Video. Video. Video. Netflix used to be just a DVD company, but now they are all about streaming video online. The technology is here for you to use video as a medium to connect with your audience. Ten years ago, the technology wasn't available to stream video on the net. Now it is. Take advantage of this and get in front of a camera, baby. If you freak out in front of the cam, get some help. Find someone. Stat.

The train is leaving the station. Are you the locomotive or the caboose? Be the locomotive.

Key takeaway: Team up with promotional partners that could set you up for some major profits. Game on.

How Much Money Do You Think You Can Make?

I'm with a group of people at one of my mastermind meetings. We are shootin' the shizzle about each of our businesses.

Then someone asks the group the big question: how much money do you want to make this year in your business? I look around at the other peeps.

I see the "deer in the headlights" look and then the answers start to come slowly . . . "Uh, I don't know. $100,000? $500,000?"

I shout back, "How about a million?" They say, "Yes! Great! Let's do it! Sure!"

Then the energy drops. I can hear all of the mental conversations. Everyone is thinking: Can I really make a lot of money? Do I really have it in me? Who am I kidding? I'll never make that kind of money.

Sometimes we are so focused on the end result that we forget that it's really all about the journey. We think that in order for us to double or triple our earnings, we have to double or triple our time at the office or do work once our kids go to bed and get up at 5:30 a.m. to check email.

We equate making more money with working even harder vs. making more money by working smarter and making an impact.

Instead of asking how much money you want to make, ask yourself how many people you want to help. That was my answer above. When I shouted out a million, it was one million people. One million entrepreneurs who struggle with their finances.

You can base your revenue goal on the amount of people you will help. Just take the pricing for your products/services and multiply it by the number of people who will buy it.

In order to do this, you must have a business model that gives you scale and leverage. Then you're off to the races.

Remember, the money will come if you can truly help people and sell your solution.

Here's my list for working smarter:

- Improve your customer experience
- Prioritize your to-do list
- Get leverage in your business
- Focus on your unique abilities and delegate the rest
- Diet, exercise, and meditate

Key takeaway: More impact = more money. How much money do you think you can make?

Hug It Out with Your Attorney

My mentor Brendon Burchard told me, "Never let your small business make you small-minded."

Think of yourself as the CEO. Every great CEO surrounds himself/herself with really bright people.

You need some smart attorneys in your corner. You need someone that can protect you from doing things the wrong way.

You probably don't think you need an attorney, but when you find out you need one, it's usually way too late. Even if you think you don't need an attorney right now, it's important to have relationships with them. You never know when you will need one.

Smart attorneys prevent problems from happening. Even though it will cost you money to hire one, the money you spend could be much lower than the money it would cost you to deal with a major problem.

And if you have to spend time and money dealing with a major problem, it will take you away from your core focus of running your business. That would stink.

Go out and network and establish relationships with a few different types of attorneys:

- A business transactional attorney (contracts and business deals)
- An employment law attorney (ask them about employee handbooks)
- An intellectual property attorney (patents/copyrights/trademarks)
- Litigation attorney (just tell them about your biz)

Here are 8 things you need to know when working with attorneys:

1. **If you work with clients, suppliers, or vendors,** an attorney can create a contract that protects you. It's better to be safe than sorry. The devil is in the details . . . CYA big time here. I can't tell you how many clients of mine have gotten screwed because they didn't have their clients sign a really good contract.

2. **Hire an attorney who specializes in the area you need.** There is only so far a general attorney can take you before he/she has to refer you out to a specialist. For example, if you need an attorney to draft contracts that you can use with your clients, don't hire a family law attorney. There are tons of attorneys that wear tons of hats. Watch out.

3. **If you hire an attorney that is a solopreneur and not part of a big firm,** you will most likely pay a lower hourly rate. While that may be great, it's important for you to know that your attorney might not have access to the resources that a larger firm does: other attorneys, more support staff, etc.

4. **Hire an attorney through a referral.** Get references and call them. Also check LinkedIn.

5. **Hire an attorney that believes in you and your business.** They need to buy into your vision and support you as you grow. Make sure they are an advocate for you and work with you. For example, if they say, "You can't do that," they should brainstorm with you to see how you *can* do that.

6. **Be very clear about what's on the clock and what's off the clock.** Most attorneys work hourly. Their time is money. If you ask them to do something, make sure you know upfront how

much it's going to cost you. The last thing you want is a financial surprise. Make sure you understand how they bill you for email communication.

7. **If you have created a product or service,** you may need to file a trademark with the US patent office. You definitely should consider working with an intellectual property attorney. After all, why not protect something that you have worked so hard to create?

8. **Who is going to do the work?** The attorney you are hiring? Their junior associate attorney? The paralegal? Their housekeeper? The cable guy? Sometimes attorneys will hand off some of the grunt work to a junior associate or paralegal. That might save you some money, but make sure that your attorney will thoroughly review the work and be actively involved with your stuff.

Key takeaway: Go out and meet with one attorney next week. Just one. You never know when you will need one in your corner.

I Didn't Know You Do That!

It's come down to this. Where have all my pillowcases gone?

I had been dreading the day that I would have to set foot in Bed Bath & Beyond (BB&B), but that day had come—they were all out of pillowcases online. Talk about dry heaving into a brown paper bag.

The bedding was on the second floor and BB&B positioned the escalator in the back of the store, so I had to walk through the store to get to the second floor.

Pretty. Freaking. Smart.

As I was heading toward the escalator (more on that in a minute), I started looking around the store and fell in love with this $20 chair cushion (it totally rocks, by the way).

BB&B's subtle marketing was spot on. They had low price point items on the outer aisles and the $20 chair cushion caught my eye. My intention was to buy pillowcases and, all of a sudden, I was buying more stuff that I didn't even know that I wanted until I saw it.

I had no idea that BB&B sold chair cushions!

Ever hear any of your clients say, "I didn't know you do that"?

You never knew that your CPA did bookkeeping.

You didn't know that your graphic designer creates custom Facebook pages.

You had no idea that your attorney could file and create an LLC for you.

Key takeaway: If your clients and customers don't know everything you do, you could be leaving money on the table. You have to give your people a 360-degree view of all of your products and services. That way, they can see everything that you have available to offer them.

But wait. There's more! Your customers need to think that they are getting a good deal. How many times do you go to Bed Bath & Beyond with one of those 20% off coupons?

I bet the whole Krane community could get 10,000% off with all of our coupons! What a deal! Make a list of all the products and services you offer (hopefully it's more than one). Make sure your clients know everything you do. Seed with stories and case studies. Get them into your "store" by marketing to them. Make them feel like they are getting a deal. Rinse and repeat.

I Fried My Bangs (Really)

I was in Kauai with my fam a few years ago. Great day in the sun, but we couldn't motivate ourselves to go out for dinner. We were all pretty beat.

So I decided to grill some chicken on one of those outdoor barbecues. Can you see where I'm going with this? Yes . . . oh man.

I put the chicken on the grill. I hit the ignition switch. I turned the knob. No flame came on. I did it again. Nothing. Oh jeez, so I leaned in just a little to check. I tried it again.

And bam!

The flame came on just enough to go through the grill and . . . burn my hair.

Disco inferno.

My hair was up in smoke. I now had no bangs *or* the bangs I had left were fried. My kids were right there and saw the whole thing. Thank G-D it just got my hair.

As soon as everyone saw that I was OK, my kids were like, "Dad, did anyone get that on video? We need to get that on *America's Funniest Home Videos*! We could win!"

What a rookie move I made. I leaned in too much and got too close to the grill.

Talk about rookie moves. I see many people making rookie moves with their money year in and year out.

One of THE biggest mistakes I see people make is that they don't put money in their IRA's (or other retirement accounts).

For IRA's, you have 2 choices.

The deadline is April 15th.

You can do a regular (traditional) IRA and you will (usually) get a tax deduction for the amount you contribute. Check with your accountant.

You can contribute up to $5,500 if you are under age 50 and $6,500 if you are over age 50. These amounts could change in the future. Ask your accountant.

You (or your spouse) need to have earned income (meaning you are working).

The money grows tax deferred and you pay taxes when you take out the money.

You need to leave the money in until age 59 ½ or there are penalties.

You can do a Roth IRA.

You are contributing after tax money, so you get no tax deduction.

You can contribute up to $5,500 if you are under age 50 and $6,500 if you are over age 50. These amounts could change in the future. Ask your accountant.

You (or your spouse) need to have earned income (meaning you are working).

The money grows tax deferred and you DON'T pay taxes when you take out the money.

You need to leave the money in until age 59 ½ or there are penalties AND taxes on any gains.

There are also income limitations on Roth IRA's, meaning that if you make over a certain amount of money, you can't contribute to a Roth. These change all of the time. Go here for the current income limits: www.irs.gov/Retirement-Plans

All of these details can be tricky. Review this stuff with your CPA. Check out the above link from the IRS. There are many little rules on IRA's.

Key takeaway: No more rookie moves. I want you to keep your bangs. Put money in your retirement account every year.

Looking for a tool to track your spending? Check out my Spending-Saving Calculator.   Just go to www.jkrane.com/mymoney. You can also go to the back of the book in the resources tab. You can get the info there as well.

Is Your Lettuce Soggy?

I t happens to the best of us. We go to a restaurant.
We get the Cobb. Or maybe the Caesar. Maybe the chopped.

All of these salads come loaded with tons of dressing. Those guys in the kitchen really pour it on! Major.

Then the salad sits on the counter while the waiter is helping someone else and you're starving, so the lettuce just gets nutso soggy.

Next thing you know, you're eating lettuce soup. What the F?

You have a few bites. It's terrible. You wish you had just ordered the dressing on the side.

That way, you would've had more control over that salad.

The lettuce would be crunchy.

You could watch your calories.

It would be awesome.

Enter the parallel to your product and service offerings.

First off, you need to give your customers some choices. That way, they can buy the stuff they want and feel like they have some control when they decide what to buy.

So how much stuff are you selling? What are your price points?

Key takeaway: Create a menu of your stuff. Give your clients some choices. I've created a pretty cool PDF to help you create a menu of your stuff.

To get the menu of money tool, just go to the back of the book in the resources page.

Magda Hit on Me

I was at the counter at La Scala—one of my favorite restaurants—eating my turkey chopped salad. Chillin' like Bob Dylan.

Just minding my own bidniz, doin' a little reading. This older lady sits down next to me, checks me out, and starts kibitzing (Yiddish for "talking") with me.

She had this major tan like Magda from *There's Something About Mary*. She totally hit on me. I know! Then she asked me to help her with her phone.

I looked at the phone and it was one of those 1995 phones that flip open where you have to hit the button 3 times to text the letter "c."

I asked her how long she'd had it and she said it was brand new! What? Do they even make those anymore?

Magda said she lost her phone charger—that she had tried to buy a new charger, but she couldn't find any, so she had to buy a new phone.

But she bought the same phone! On purpose. She said it was easier to text with. Really?

She didn't upgrade and get a smart phone. She settled for the same 1995 old school one.

Some people stick with the same stuff for *way* too long, but when they aren't getting what they pay for—like, no value—that means it's time to upgrade.

I'm no Stanford MBA grad. I don't manage $4 billion dollars. I'm not 72 years old with 48 years of experience. I don't work in the ultra-high-net-worth private wealth management blah, blah, blah firm.

But I've been around the block, working with over 75 entrepreneurs in the last 5 years. I've created specific, detailed, strategic plans for them. One of THE major challenges for them has been no tax planning. Like NONE. Zero.

I'm tellin' ya one thing to upgrade right now: your accountant. Move on and upgrade if you aren't getting the proactive planning you deserve.

If you don't do tax projections, you get surprises. The good surprises are when you get money back.

The bad ones are when you owe a ton of dough. I, literally, have heard 3 people say that they owe over $10k in taxes—and they were surprised. Their CPA never called them to do any tax planning. What a dud.

Key takeaway: It's so much better to pay your taxes as you go rather than all at once. That's what I do and what I tell my clients to do. But the thing is, you need to know how much you owe—and immediately get on a plan.

Knowing = clarity = feeling organized = able to breathe.

One more thing: Don't think a CPA is only good if they get you money back. The numbers don't lie.

McDonalds and Subway
Have This. Do You?

According to the U.S. Dept. of Commerce, 95% of franchises are still in business after 5 years. According to the Bureau of Labor Statistics and the SBA, only 50% of small businesses survive within 5 years.

So why do franchises stay in business longer? They follow a system. A step-by-step system to run their business.

This system is in an operations manual. The franchisor creates it for them.

An operations manual is a written plan for how to run your biz. It should be written so that a complete stranger could walk into your building and take over the duties of any job you've hired your employees to do.

If you're an entrepreneur, think about why you got into business for yourself. You wanted freedom and autonomy. You wanted to do things your way, create value, and get paid well for it. So why not write all of this stuff down?!

Here's what an operations manual can do for you:

1. **High quality and less room for error.** Having these systems in writing will keep the quality of your product/service consistently high. The key is the consistency, because the steps are documented in the manual. This will also eliminate the amount of mistakes that your employees could make.

2. **Better use of your time.** Ever feel like you would rather work from home than go into the office because there are fewer interruptions? Say goodbye to your employees interrupting you every 20 minutes with questions. Tell them the answers are in the manual. If they aren't, then put them there! That's what I do. Now that you have systems that are written down and documented, you should have more time to focus on sales, marketing, and any other strategic initiatives you want to do. That's where the real growth occurs. Seriously.

3. **Your business could be more attractive to a buyer.** Maybe you'll get a higher price for your company because you have written policies and procedures in place. Buyers love that kind of stuff. They want to buy a well-oiled machine.

An operations manual should include 2 main things:

1. **All of the company information that you would want any new or existing employee to know.** Some examples include: product/service offerings, vendor contact info, username/passwords, and emergency contact info.

2. **Every system and procedure for each type of employee to follow.** An example of a procedure is a checklist that your employees should follow when using your company's CRM database software.

Your manual needs to be alive—no more fungus and mold on top of that manual!

It should have a heartbeat. Always update your manual. There is never too much info that you can't add to it.

Go out and create one or update the one you have.

I want you to be in business 10 years from now. Let's go!

Key takeaway: Create an operations manual. Write out how specific things are done on a step-by-step basis. That way, your biz can be streamlined and you won't freak out if you lose an employee. Why? Because everything will be documented.

Should Guys Get Spray Tans?

When the ladies get them, they look real. But when guys get spray tans, they look like Magda's twin brother from the movie *There's Something About Mary*.

Spray tans last about 7 to 12 days, so if you're into this stuff, you have to go every 1-2 weeks. That's a lot of tanning and that's money you spend, every week.

So that is a recurring fixed expense for you. Maybe that's where all your money goes.

Do you ever ask yourself: Where does all the money go? Why do I feel like I have no money?

You think you're killing it in your business, right? You're bringing in the biz. You think you're making good money.

But every month when you look at your business bank account, there isn't that much cash in there.

Every business owner spends money in 2 areas:

The money you spend to produce/provide a service or product, which is called costs of goods sold.

The money you spend to keep your business up and running, which is called overhead.

Stay with me here. You really need to understand this.

It's so key to get a handle on your business money. You will have more clarity. You will feel more in control. You could go to the moon! Seriously.

Here's an example:

Let's say you're an event planner and you're planning a business conference for a client. Your fee is $100,000.

You will supply and pay for the event production, including the flowers, tables, chairs, catering, and staff. You plan for all the expenses to cost $70,000, so you plan to make $30,000, or 30% profit. The $30,000 is called your gross profit.

Gross profit = revenue – cost of goods sold

But the event ends up costing you $85,000. You are over budget, so your gross profit is only $15,000.

You also have overhead to run your business. You have to pay for rent, health insurance, your employees, and the telephones in your office. This costs $8,000 every month.

Net profit = gross profit – overhead

So in this case, your net profit is $15,000 – $8,000 = $7,000.

That's it, you made just $7,000 off of $100,000 in sales! Oy vey. We've gotta get this number up.

If we annualize this, your net profit for the year would be $84,000.

The thing is, you left your corporate job where you were making $80,000, so you're basically making the same amount of money.

Yes, you have more autonomy. You have your own company. You have more flexibility. But you are really making the same amount of money.

Key takeaway: Something has to change. You have 3 choices:

1. Raise your prices.
2. Lower the costs to produce the event. You could lower the costs to make/provide your service or product and stay on budget.
3. Lower your overhead.

It's that simple. You make the decision then run with it—just not to the tanning salon every week.

Tesla — Talk of the Town

Tesla. I don't want to mess with ya. You are the talk of the town. The stores are filled with people wanting to buy you. Your CEO Elon Musk is a stud. Super smart guy.

Why are Tesla cars the talk of the town? Here are 5 things we entrepreneurs can learn from the success of Tesla Motors:

1. **Be innovative.** Design a product or perform a service that speaks for itself. If your stuff flat out rocks, it will make marketing it so much easier (so less stressful!).

   Word of mouth is HUGE.

   CEO Elon Musk said, "Never produce a bad product." He even discontinued the Tesla Roadster because he couldn't stand "100%" behind it. The Tesla car is beautiful. It's sleek. The interior is amazing, with all sorts of technology that comes with it. People say it is wicked fast. When people take it for a test drive, they are blown away by how cool it is.

   Consumer Reports magazine gave it a score of 99 out of 100. They even went so far to say that it is the best car in the world. Driving a Tesla makes people think that they are taking part in the wave of the future. Everyone who owns one tells their friends how cool their car is.

2. **Get strategic partners**—wait—get the *right* strategic partners.

Ever hear the expression 1+1=3? When you align your business with the right people, it is so much easier to take your business to the moon. I'm talkin' growing exponentially.

The deal is, you need to find these people and seek them out (try social media and live events).

Tesla has 4 key strategic partners. The first two are the federal government and each state in the US (at the time I wrote this!). The feds will give you a $7,500 tax credit if you buy a car. The state of California will give you a $2,500 credit as well. (Review this info with your tax professional and check here as well):

www.teslamotors.com/incentives/US/California

Tesla is using "other people's" money to make itself more affordable to the mass market. The 3rd and 4th partners are Tesla's financing partners: U.S. Bank and Wells Fargo.

They have extended the financing period. Now your monthly payment goes down.

Tesla has even said that they guarantee a resale value of 50% of the purchase price of the Model S car.

Elon Musk is even giving his own personal guarantee. He wants Tesla to have the highest resale value of any luxury sedan. He is putting his own money behind it. How's that for a guarantee?

3. **Diversify your product line.** Don't just sell one thing. This may help you smooth out the ups and downs of your cash flow. Think about what else you could sell to your customer or an adjacent target market that may be interested in what else you have to offer.

Tesla is also an OEM (original equipment manufacturer). They sell batteries to Daimler for its Smartcars. Tesla's core business is selling cars, but they have found a way to diversify their sales.

4. **Make your product or service serve a greater social cause.** If people feel that your product can help a greater cause rather than

just themselves, they will be really motivated to buy it. People want to change the world and can really get inspired when they are participating in something bigger than themselves.

Many people think that the Tesla cars are friendlier to the environment. No gas, all electric—zero fuel emissions. (I know there are reports about greater use of electricity and people talk about what Tesla is going to do with all of those batteries. But the bottom line is that many people think that buying electric cars is better for the environment.)

5. **Save your clients money.** People will spend money if they feel that they could save money down the road. The more money people could save, and the longer they could save the money, the more motivated they will be to buy your stuff.

The Tesla car is all-electric and drivers don't use gas, they just recharge at super charging stations. So in the customer's mind, they feel like they could save $50-$300 bucks a month depending on how much they drive.

So these are my 5 ideas. Pick a few of them or just pick one and take massive action!

Key takeaway: Brendon Burchard, one of my mentors, said, "Never let your small business make you small-minded." Put your foot on your business's Tesla accelerator. Think big. Ready, set, go!

The Hump on Your Own Back

M y grandma used to say, "Justin, you can't see the hump on your own back."

I love that line. I still use it today. It's really a good one when there is a problem or opportunity right under our noses—especially when running a business.

Sometimes we are too close to the problems in our business.

We can't even see them. We're outta touch, Hall & Oats style.

It could be the lack of systems, the fact that we're playing too small, or that we're not paying enough attention to our clients. It takes an outsider to identify them to us. Then we have to get out of denial (major denial) and view these problems as opportunities to take our business to the next level.

This stuff isn't easy. You have to look at yourself. Believe me, I'm a super big violator and am trying to get better. You're not the only one that might need an intervention.

Let's drill down a little deeper. Let's focus on your relationships with your clients and customers. Think about your last 3 clients that were unhappy or had a beef about something. What were they unhappy about? Was it just them? Or you? Maybe a combo? Have you been unaware of the same problem happening over and over? Is there anything you think you can do to improve?

Put yourself in their shoes. See what their issue is from their point of view. Validate their feelings and make them feel heard. Unhappy customers can shed some major light on what you need to improve in your business.

Maybe there's a solution that you can implement and use across the board in your business. Talk about a game changer.

You can never completely get rid of the hump on your back, so here are 5 things you can do to be more AWARE of what's going on in your business:

1. **Hire an outside business consultant.** Have them just observe what you do for a few days. Let them interview you and your staff. Be open to hearing what they say and be willing to see it as an opportunity for growth and change!
2. **Join a mastermind.** Tell others about your business. Develop relationships with them. Use them as your virtual focus group. I run one.
3. **Survey your clients and customers.** Ask them what they like and what they don't like. Get a little intel about what's going on.
4. **Spy on your competition.** Especially people or companies above your level. What are they specifically doing or not doing? How do you compare?
5. **Take your spouse, close friend, or significant other out to dinner.** Tell them what you're up to. Tell them where you feel stuck. They know you very well. They don't have to know your business inside and out. They could be a resource for you.

Key takeaway: You don't know what you don't know. The key is to get an outsider's point of view. We gotta get you to see the hump on your own back. Then you'll be aware of what you can do to be a more successful entrepreneur.

This Ever Happened to You?

I bet this has happened to you.

You bring your bedhead in the a.m. to the kitchen.

At around 7:30 a.m. you have your morning coffee/tea. You check email and start to reply to a few of them. The minutes are ticking by. Next thing you know, it's 9:00 a.m.

Then your cell phone rings and it's a big referral source. You take the call but your cell phone dies. Now they are calling you on Skype. You click "answer with video," but you forget that you are still in your PJ's with your yucky T-shirt and major bad hair!

Oy vey. Where did the time go?

Do you ever feel like sometimes you work at home and never make it into the office?

Do you sometimes think that you should ditch your office and just work out of your house? You could save some serious money, such as no rent and maybe some tax deductions.

Before we get into the economics of home office vs. regular office, you need to think of a few things about having a home office as your primary place of business.

If you have other people in your house, like crazy wild kids, its going to be pretty hard for you to get things done, unless you have a separate (presidential) wing where you can go. You need a quiet space.

If you worked at home, would you have that cabin fever feeling and feel like you need to get out of the house?

Would you find it hard to separate working at home from shutting down and relaxing at home?

There are 4 key ways that you save money if you work from home:

1. No rent.
2. Less gas because you're not driving to work.
3. Eating from home. It's usually cheaper.
4. Potential tax deductions. Remember to consult your tax professional for advice specific to your situation.

Attention smart money-saving tax peeps:

The IRS has specific rules as to whether you can claim some tax deductions from working at home.

You must regularly use part of your home for exclusively doing business.

You also need to show the IRS that your home is your principal place of business.

Click here for all the details: www.irs.gov/Businesses/Small-Businesses-&-Self-Employed/Home-Office-Deduction

The current way to take a home office deduction is to fill out form 8829. It has 43 lines of financial stuff that you/your CPA fills out. You have to figure out what percentage of your house your office makes up. Then you have to put in all of your expenses like mortgage interest, utilities, and property taxes. It's like baking a cake!

The key is, you have to track all of your expenses for the year, keep financial records, and then give it to your CPA. Tons of work, but it could be worth it.

The IRS is giving you a simpler way to take a home office deduction. The catch is, the cap is $1,500. It boils down to a $5 per square foot deduction with a cap of 300 square feet.

Click here for the deets: www.irs.gov/Businesses/Small-Businesses-&-Self-Employed/Simplified-Option-for-Home-Office-Deduction

Key takeaway: If you are working from home, part-time or full-time, or considering doing the home office thang, call your accountant and see how much money you could save in taxes. Once you know this, estimate how much you would save in rent, gas, and food.

Now you could have some extra money to invest, pay down debt, or use in your biz. Yes, I have a normal office, but I'm writing this from home with my bedhead and coffee! Is it just me, or do we all wake up with wild hair?

What's Your Return on Fun?

O nce I hung out with David Beckham.

We were both watching our kids play soccer. I had a chance to ask David what soccer taught him. He told me that playing soccer and achieving his level of success was just about one word:

FUN.

As soon as he started having fun and enjoying what he was doing, the results came.

That got me thinking, what's your rate of return on having fun? How much fun are you having in your business?

What if the unit of currency was fun instead of dollars? What if we used that fun currency to buy and sell things? How cool would that be?

Once you start having fun in your business, the results start coming.

It took me 13 years to realize this. When I was a financial advisor at a professional Wall Street firm, I didn't have that much fun. It was boring. I wasn't enjoying myself. Not that much laughing. I got into this routine and ultimately felt stuck.

Can you have some more fun in your business?

Here are 4 things you can do to have more fun as a business owner:

1. **Do the things you love to do!** Ya know, the stuff your clients pay you for! The things you could do all day long because it's your passion and what you're good at.

   Delegate some of the other things that you're competent at but that anyone can do. You'll feel better. If you don't, take two Advil and call me in the morning.

2. **Recharge and rejuvenate.** Take a day off from work. Take a nap, go to the movies, do some laughing, yoga, play the Wii. Disconnect from your phone.

   When you come back to the office, you will feel better and enjoy your work that much more.

3. **Work with employees, coworkers, clients, and vendors who are positive,** easy to get along with, creative, and fun. It's very hard to work with people who suck the energy out of you. Can I get a high five here?

4. **Make the decision.** Really? Just decide. Yes! Once you decide that you want more fulfillment and enjoyment out of your day, you're halfway there.

Key takeaway: You must have fun in your business. Otherwise, you will get burned out. You'll be tired and stale. Go out and have some fun at the office. Ever go to a laughing party? Try hosting one. It's hilarious!

White Zin & Lipstick

I had no idea about these two.
The fact that they both can be used for something else.

Maybe it's because I'm a guy. And maybe it's because I don't really like Cabernet wine.

So check me out on this.

I'm having a drink with a client and he orders a Cab. He tastes it and really doesn't like it. It's too strong, too big, too much for him, so he asks the waiter to bring over a bissel (Yiddish for "little") of White Zinfandel.

My client pours the Zin into the Cab, and voila! He said it tasted so much better. Even I tried it. It was pretty good. Vino, baby.

I had no idea that if you put a little White Zinfandel into a Cab, that it takes the edge off and makes the Cab taste better. Where did that come from? It's nutzo.

Later that night, I'm in the car with some friends and we're running late to a dinner party.

All of a sudden, one of my friends starts putting lipstick on her face and then she starts rubbing it in. I'm like, what?! Lipstick on your cheeks? She says, "Yes, when we women are in a bind, we use lipstick as blush."

Oh man, am I out of touch. Where did that come from?

Got me thinking, the little things in life—they can be used for more than one thing.

So why can't we take our existing assets in our business, leverage them, and use them in other ways? To make more money and be more profitable, y'all!

Zinfandel style. Lipstick style.

So here's my list of some assets you probably have in your business that you can use in other ways.

1. **Your content.** Turn a blogpost into a podcast and throw it on iTunes. Convert a blogpost into a video and put it on YouTube. I'm definitely going to do it with this post.

2. **Your relationships.** Your network is your net worth. Go back through your Rolodex and re-establish old connections. Turn them into successful JV (joint venture) partners for you.

3. **Technology.** Are you using any type of CRM software? Where do you store your leads, prospects, and client info? My guess is that you're using some type of software and that you aren't using all it has to offer. Use Google Analytics. Try Evernote. Check out Dropbox. All of these tools could make you more productive.

4. **SBDC's (small business development centers) in your area.** These are organizations backed by federal money, state money, and private sector funds. Some examples are the SBA and SCORE. Did I mention that they are free?

5. **Office space.** If you rent office space, sometimes you get free conference room space from your landlord. Make use of it and invite a group of people to do informal networking there. Make it a potluck thing.

6. **Your vendors.** They are really good relationships that you already have. Have them sponsor you/your company for something. Just pick up the phone and ask them for help.

7. **Business books you've already read.** Go back and re-read them. You will pick up on new ideas and take action in different ways. I just re-read the *E-Myth Revisited.* Again. For the third time.

There are tons of other things you can do. Think about all the things at your fingertips. Use them in new ways.

As business owners, we are all in this together. Sometimes I can't even create my way out of a paper bag.

But at least we know about White Zin and lipstick.

Key takeaway: Be strategic with the assets that you already have.

Who Is Going to Take Fred, Your Pet Goat?

Your pet goat, Fred.

Fred's been with you for a long time, but you have to get rid of him. You're moving and can't take him with you. Boy, are you going to miss Fred—his bad breath, selling his goat milk, and using him as a lawnmower.

So who are you going to sell Fred to? And how much is he worth?

What if Fred was your business? A lucrative business you've had for a while.

There are so many ways you can sell Fred. You can sell him outright to a buyer. Or maybe you do a merger with another pet goat company.

In either case, finding the right buyer is key.

Why? Because if you sell your company to a buyer who doesn't share your values, your clients/customers will leave.

And if you care about what happens to your clients after you're gone, then selling to a buyer who shares your values is really important.

One great way to assure a smooth transition is to bring in a partner before you plan to sell. Another option is to make a key employee a partner by giving him/her equity.

You could also work with a business broker. Or you could spread the word through your contacts such as your attorney, CPA, and any other trusted advisor who might know a buyer worthy of your business.

The value of your business is usually determined by your results over the last 3 years.

There are two key things that will determine the value of your business, if you have a service-based business.

1. **Transition risk of client base.** The easier you are able to transition your clients to the buyer, the more your business is worth. For example, say you do business with your clients on a face-to-face basis, but you find out your potential buyer solely does business over the phone. Obviously, this is not a good match.
2. **Your cash flow.** Your revenue stream needs to be as predictable as possible. You also want to make sure that you don't have only a few clients who make up a big portion of your revenue. Also, the age range of your client base needs to be as diverse as possible. This creates a more long-lasting revenue stream.

Here is a possible math scenario for selling your business. Read this over a few times. If your eyes glaze over this, go get a glass of wine and read it a few times. Seriously. Talk it out with yourself.

Let's assume your last 12 months of sales are $250,000 and that you've decided to sell your ownership to a junior person at your company.

Let's say the sale price is $500,000.

You could ask for 20% down or $100,000.

You could then issue a promissory note for $175,000. You are basically lending the buyer the $175k and he/she is making monthly payments, say at a rate of 6%, for a period of 4 years.

So you now know exactly how much money you will get paid every month.

A third and final phase of the deal is called an earn-out. The buyer pays the seller a percentage of the future revenue for an agreed upon period of time. In this case, the buyer has paid $275,000 and is still on the hook for another $225,000.

The buyer can pay the seller 10% of the seller's revenues after each year. This motivates the seller to successfully transition the clients to the new buyer. The use of this earn-out may increase or decrease the final purchase price.

The tax treatment in all of these types of sales varies. Many of these sales can allow the seller to use long-term capital gains tax rates and not ordinary income tax rates on the sale. (Please consult your tax professional for more information.)

Bear in mind that this is only one way that you could structure a deal to sell your pet goat. There many, many other ways you can structure the transition to achieve the outcome you want.

Key takeaway: Make your business a lucrative one that's attractive to potential buyers. Develop a plan to monetize the value of it. Your customers will continue to be taken care of and you could be handsomely rewarded.

I see so many entrepreneurs close up shop and leave huge money on the table. Fred, your pet goat, is worth something. He could be your ticket to a sweet lifestyle down the road.

You Already Know This

Y ou can't build an empire all by yourself. You can't wear all the hats in your business.

You'd drive yourself crazy trying to grow your business.

But you know this. So chances are, you've either hired some employees or you've been mulling it over.

Either way, here are 5 things to put on your must-do list when hiring employees:

1. **Create an employee handbook.** I am not an employment attorney and I'm not the caped crusader, or Carnac from *The Johnny Carson Show*, but I do know that having an employee handbook can protect you. I have written about this before. It outlines employee duties, your expectations, and basically makes things really clear between you and your employees. A handbook can cost anywhere between $1,000 and $2,500 if an attorney creates it. However, I'm sure your uncle could do it for $300.

2. **Create a process for hiring employees.** Ask yourself what type of person you are trying to hire. Are you looking for a creative

type or a details person? Do you want someone who is right-brain oriented? Or are you trying to hire a systems person?

One way to cut through all this is to have potential employees take the Kolbe A Index. It may be the best $50 you spend, besides a chopped salad at La Scala in Beverly Hills. The test screens for 4 qualities, 3 of which are really important ones: fact finder, follow through, and quick start. Hire the right person the first time rather than spending time training the wrong person, letting them go, and doing it all over again.

3. **Calculate the cost of contributing to your employees' company retirement account.** If your employees will be full-time and you have a retirement plan like a 401k, SEP IRA, or profit sharing plan, you will have to contribute some dough into their retirement account.

For example, if you contribute $20,000 to your own 401k, you may have to contribute $6,000 to your employees' 401k as well. (These are totally made up numbers. Just trying to give you an example. Ask a pension consultant or actuary.) Don't just look at the numbers. Look at the bigger picture because this is a good thing for you. It will help you recruit, retain, and reward your employees.

4. **Workers compensation insurance.** If your employees get hurt on the job, this type of insurance pays for medical expenses and part of their lost wages. The state of California, along with many others, makes this a mandatory requirement for employers. This insurance is just a cost of doing business. You have to foot the bill. The nature of your business will determine what the premium will be.

5. **Payroll taxes.** As a business owner, you are responsible for paying employer payroll taxes. These payroll taxes are an extra expense over and above what you pay your employees. The employer portion of payroll taxes include the following:

Social Security taxes (6.2% up to the annual maximum)

Medicare taxes (1.45% of wages)

Federal unemployment taxes (FUTA)
State unemployment taxes (SUTA)

Then there are FICA Taxes. FICA stands for the Federal Insurance Contributions Act. The FICA tax consists of both Social Security and Medicare taxes. Social Security and Medicare taxes are paid both by the employees and the employer. Both parties pay half of these taxes. Together, both halves of the FICA taxes add up to 15.3%. The 15.3% FICA tax is broken down as follows:

Social Security (Employee pays 6.2%)
Social Security (Employer pays 6.2%)
Medicare (Employee pays 1.45%)
Medicare (Employer pays 1.45%)
Source: www.taxes.about.com

Key takeaway: You already know this, but you can't do everything yourself in business. So many people hire virtual assistants and independent contractors. That's fine.

But at some point, as you are really growing, you will be faced with hiring employees. People that are dedicated to working just for you. Use these 5 points above to know what the true costs are when you hire an employee.

You Are So Bieber

Justin Bieber + Leverage = Biebage.

Leverage. One of the biggest words you need to focus on in business. It's about getting the best bang for your buck *or* the best use of your time.

Think about how Bieber used leverage to become so popular and successful.

His mother uploaded his videos to YouTube. Anyone could watch them. People began to like him and his mother continued to post more videos. He created a following through the biggest leverage point ever, the Internet, which allowed him to reach a ton of people.

He then signed a record deal with Usher, a well-known R&B artist who had a record label. Usher gave Bieber a platform (more Biebage) to launch his career.

You could be Bieber too! How did he get his hair to go that way? Seriously? Aqua Net? Hair gel?

I've already told you the definition of insanity: doing the same thing over and over again and hoping for a different result. You need more leverage. You need a better return for your time and money.

Think about some of the things that you can do in your business that could give you *way* better results—for just a little more work or money.

That's what leverage is all about!

Here are a few ideas on how to gain some leverage:

1. **Give presentations**, and give them to a larger audience.
2. **Raise your prices.** I'm giving you a gentle nudge to do it. You are worth it.
3. **Increase your investment in marketing.** According to a survey run by Michael Zipursky, 53% of consultants spend less than $2,000 on marketing. That seems too low.
4. **Spend more time on marketing.** Block out 1 or 2 days. Focus.
5. **Tie your employees' compensation to their performance.** Make sure the performance creates more revenue for you.
6. **Vary your pricing.** Give your customers choice. Some people might not know what they want to buy from you, but if they see it in some sort of context (with options), it might be easier for them to buy from you. It's so simple and has worked for me.
7. **Wow your prospects.** First impressions matter. What does your website look like? How are you dressed? What do people think of you and your stuff when they see you?
8. **Create bonuses.** Give away free add-ons when people buy your stuff. It builds serious goodwill.
9. **Do joint ventures.** Team up with people that serve similar customers. You can do this!

Key takeaway: We gotta get you some Biebage. In order to have a serious breakthrough in your business, you must get leverage. Otherwise, you will be stuck, making the same money. Wanna get some leverage? From time to time, I open up slots to work with me on your personal or business money. Just go to the back of the book and check out the resources section.

You Have to Buy It
Before It Happens

You're a physical therapist with your own business. You're crushin' it in your biz and then—boom! Outta nowhere, one of your old clients sends you a letter and is suing you. Oh man! He's suing you because he tripped and fell inside your waiting room.

Your heart's racing, you know you did nothing wrong, but the last thing you need is to deal with a lawsuit. This guy turned out to be a real nut. What a joker! Major oy vey.

Now you gotta deal with this lunatic.

The last thing you want is to hire an attorney that will charge you $300 for a 10-minute phone call to defend you.

We are busy enough with work, taking care of our kids, and going to Whole Foods every day.

So you call your attorney and he asks you if you have business liability insurance. You're thinking: did I ever buy that? Time stops. You remember reading about it, but you know you never got around to buying it.

You nearly s**t your pants.

I don't want this to be you.

You are working your tush off, and a really bad lawsuit can put you out of biz.

Really. Like double really.

As a business owner, you most likely need business liability insurance.

Business liability insurance protects you from liability arising from accidents, injuries, libel, and slander. The policies also cover the legal fees to defend the lawsuit. Some of your vendors or customers may even require you to have this before they do business with you.

There are different types of business liability insurance you can buy. If you sell a product, then you most likely need product liability insurance. If you're in a service-based business, then maybe you just need a general business liability policy or maybe you need professional liability insurance.

Attention home-based business owners! Work out of your house? Most homeowner's policies will not cover liabilities or losses from your business activities.

Here's what you can do to protect yourself as an entrepreneur:

Get a referral for an insurance broker. They are independent insurance professionals and can shop the best policy from the best insurance company that's right for you. If you go to your local State Farm, Farmers, or Allstate agent, they may be able to offer it to you, but they can only sell you their company's policy.

Tell your insurance broker the nature of your business. Ask him/her to identify your potential exposure, should you ever have to pay a claim.

Do 25 jumping jacks. You still reading this?

Tell your insurance broker what your sales and profits are.

How much does this stuff cost? I have seen policies cost under $1,000 a year for $1 million dollars of coverage. It's not that expensive. Review this with your insurance broker. The devil is in the details.

Key takeaway: You need to seriously consider getting business liability insurance.

You Stink at Baking Cakes?

B aking cakes.

All you need to do is follow the instructions. I don't know about you, but I stink at baking cakes. I either burn them or undercook them.

Even though the directions are right in front of me!

I'm no Mario Batali, Wolfgang Puck, or Rachel Ray.

But what I do know how to do is how to bake a CLIENT MONEY SALES CAKE.

We are going to analyze your sales from your existing client base. Let's understand what your numbers are telling you.

So get your funky money apron on and let's get to work.

You can do this in Excel or on a legal pad.

Step 1: In one column, make a list of all your client relationships. Just write their last names down.

Step 2: In the next column, write down how much revenue you are getting from each client.

Step 3: Total all the sales from each client.

Step 4: Calculate the percent of your overall revenue you're generating from each client. Take the sales from each client and divide it by the total revenue.

For example, Mr. Smith pays you $5,000. Your total sales are $50,000. So, $5,000/$50,000 = 10%. Now you know Mr. Smith makes up 10% of your total sales.

Step 5: Calculate the average revenue you are getting from each client. Divide the total sales by the number of clients you have.

If your sales are $50,000 and you have 25 clients, your average revenue per client is $50,000/25 = $2,000.

Look at those numbers. What are they telling you?

In a perfect world, no client should make up more than 10% of your revenue. You don't want 5 clients to make up 70% of your business. Depending on just a few clients is never a good idea because if you lose one of them, you could be in serious trouble.

If your business model is to provide a service to one client at a time, think about how many clients you can realistically handle. Do you currently have too many clients or not enough? Is your average price per client too low?

If you need more clients, evaluate what you are doing with:

- Your marketing plan
- Your mindset
- Time management
- Productivity/technology
- Referral sources/joint ventures

Once you know how many more clients you can handle, pick how many clients you want to bring in for the year, then multiply the average revenue per client by the number you will bring in. Voila! You have a revenue goal for this year.

If you have too many clients, you have some choices:

1. Bring in someone to help you service them.
2. Let some clients go.
3. Raise your prices to get some revenue growth.
4. Start thinking about generating passive or leveraged income.

Key takeaway: Read this money recipe over a few times. This post is a total keeper. It's one of my best. You don't have to bake a perfect cake. Just get moving and make some progress.

You Won't Regret This

T hose Wetzel's Pretzels people got me!

I'm walking in the mall, minding my own business, and there they are—those pretzel sample people.

I take a free sample, my kids take one too, and the next thing I know, I'm buying 3 pretzels and 3 strawberry lemonades for $17!

I went from taking a free sample to buying something.

What's going on here?!

By getting a taste (for free), I get a chance to see/feel/experience what I would get if I bought the whole thing (or more). I got to try it out to see if I liked it.

The last thing I want to do is have buyer's remorse. I don't want to regret the fact that I bought something that I shouldn't have. Is it just me, or do you think this way too?

Business lesson: You need to make your customers feel like they won't regret buying your stuff.

By trying something out for free, your customers get a taste of what it would be like to work with you or buy your product. It could be a free consultation or a sample of your product.

Obviously, you don't want to work for free. You need to get paid. You're going to need to convert your free offers into sales.

Would you buy a car without test driving it?

People are more willing to try you out for free or for a few bucks rather than spend a bunch of money. Once they see value, they believe they won't regret buying your more expensive stuff.

The question is, do you offer different services at different price points?

This is why you need a product/service funnel for your business.

The funnel is a way for you to strategically, over time, take your clients through different product/service offerings, from free/low-price points to higher price points.

The Wetzel's Pretzels people got me here with that free sample.

Sometimes it's also easier to convert people that have bought your lower-priced items to buy your higher-priced items than it is to simply convert prospects into buying your higher priced offerings.

Here is how your funnel should look from a pricing standpoint: free, low-price, mid-price, high-price. That's it. It's that simple.

Having a funnel benefits two people: you and your customer.

You: It's an easy way to back into your sales goal. You just list out the price points and multiply by how many sales you have to make in each category. You need to be tracking this stuff. The funnel forces you to do this. May the Force be with you on this one.

Your customer/client: They won't feel like they're going to regret buying your stuff. You want them to feel that, in hindsight, they made the right decision. It could make them come back for more!

Key takeaway: Make your customers feel like they won't regret buying your stuff.

Your Biz. Paying Dividends?

D ividends Schmividends!   It's one of the best investment strategies out there.

Investing in companies that have the ability to raise their dividends is huge. Stay with me on this one because there is a key lesson here on what this means for your own business and its valuation.

What is a dividend? A company has profits. Sometimes they reinvest the profits back into their business and then they can choose to pay the rest out to shareholders.

The rest of that money that is paid out is called a dividend.

If you buy stock in a company that raises the dividend over time, that's an incremental amount of money you would get each year. It's like being a kid and getting a bigger allowance every year on your birthday.

Check out this hypothetical example:

Let's say you bought stock in Automatic Data Processing (ADP), the payroll company, at $42 in January 2008.

In 2008, it paid a dividend of $1.16 per share. So that is a 2.70% yield. Here's the math: 1.16/42 = 2.70%

Every year, ADP has raised its dividend, meaning it grew its business enough each year to be able to afford to pay shareholders a larger dividend.

At the time of this article, the dividend is expected to be $1.74, so ADP has raised the dividend from $1.16 to $1.74. That is a 50% increase from the dividend you were getting back in 2008.

So you were making 2.70% on your money. But now, because ADP has raised its dividend, you are now making 4.70% on your money.

Here's the math: 1.74/42 = 4.70%

Source: Automatic Data Processing, Investor Relations

Dividends are one of the simplest ways to value a stock. In the above example, it's one of the main reasons why the ADP stock price (as I write this) is at $73!

Remember, dividends are just cash flow payments that you get as a shareholder.

Who doesn't want their business to be worth as much as possible?

How about we think of your business as a stock?

You have revenue, expenses, and profits. When I say profits, I'm referring to how much money your company makes after your business expenses.

Your business MUST make money.

That's the money we can consider to be dividend money.

The larger the dividend, and the more it increases over time, the more your business could be worth.

There are 2 ways you could grow your company's dividend:

1. Grow sales
2. Cut expenses

If you plan on selling your business to fund your retirement or just cashing out, you need to show this rising dividend stuff to an investor. It could make your biz worth way more.

Who wouldn't want to invest in a business where the ROI increases over time?

Key takeaway: Just because your business is private doesn't mean that you can't think of your business as a public company. Yes, you don't have to answer to shareholders, but you still have to answer to the largest shareholder in the world—you!

Your Pool Guy Is a Stud

Your pool guy, your cable company, your gym, and your dry cleaner—they've totally got you.

I mean, think about it: You don't use them just once. You use them on a recurring basis and every month you pay them.

Talk about a killer business model! Total cash cows, right?

No matter what business you're in, the longer you get paid, the better. You have to make your client/customer feel like your product or service is a must-have so they will stay with you. Forevs.

At my live event this week, I talked about a bunch of ways to increase your business revenue. Everyone loved the idea to just keep a client longer or to sell a product that people buy more than just one time.

I have clients who pay their personal trainers hundreds of dollars a week! They can easily go to the gym on their own and schvitz (Yiddish for "sweat"), but they don't because they see the benefit that their personal trainer provides.

Check this out. Let's say you're a nutritionist and you have 50 clients. You have a 3-month program, which is $300 a month. So that's $900 per client multiplied by 50 clients = $45,000 in revenue. If you just doubled the program from 3 months to 6 months, there would be an extra 45 G's! Hello travel budget!

What would you have to do to double the amount of time your client stays with you? How are you going to propose this to your client or customer?

Try this: make your offer around saving money, making more money, saving time, or making your client feel better for a longer period of time. You then need to articulate the increased value that your customer is getting.

Are you the one doing all the work to service your clients? If you want to keep your clients for longer, that means you will eventually go from working a 10-hour day to a 13-hour day. Oy vey.

Create more capacity to handle the additional work. Try removing yourself from every single client touch point. Hire staff to help you. Leverage technology to make yourself more productive. You've got the money now because you just increased your revenue.

Key takeaway: Make your revenue stream more like an annuity. It's so much easier to keep an existing client/customer than to find a new one. The longer they stay with you, the more impact you will make on their lives and the longer you will get paid. Cha-ching! That way, you could spend more time doing your vision work, your strategy stuff, and working on your business.

Your Business:
A Game Changer for Your Money—
Action Plan Part One

Y ou must think big. I want you to make decisions based on where you want to be—not where you are.

It's time for your business to grow. I mean really grow. The train is leaving the station, baby, and you need to hop on board.

Why? Because you are AMAZING!

You are awesome.

The key is, you must run your business where you are the best version of yourself.

So I have some questions for you:

1. Why are you in business to begin with?
2. What is it about your business that lights you up?
3. What really motivates you?
4. Do you really believe in what you are doing?
5. Do you believe in you?

Write down your answers. You need to stay in this space, this happy, positive space.

If you are not in this mindset, it will be hard for you to take action, to implement these nuggets I'm giving you.

Take some time to answer these questions. Do it for yourself.

Your Business:
A Game Changer for Your Money—
Action Plan Part Two

Financial freedom. Financial independence.

Having enough money to do what you want, when you want, and not having to rely on anyone else for help.

How cool is that?!

Money doesn't buy happiness, but it sure makes things easier. When you use money in ways that align with your values, you're in a place where you get a return on life.

I see so many people leave a corporate job for a better work/life balance, but then they end up working harder and making the same money or even less.

You don't have to work an 18-hour day to be successful in business.

You just have to be smart with how you structure your business *and* your time.

You need to set up your business to make you money.

It's so hard to grow when you ONLY work one-on-one or trade hours for dollars.

Your business needs **scale and leverage**. From the beginning. I wish I knew that when I started out. Ha!

Scale happens when you don't have to spend more money to make more money. It's where you spend the same amount of money and make more money.

Leverage is where you gain success by doing more with less.

Write down a list of the top 3 things that you sell or offer. It doesn't matter if you're a product-based business or service-based. Just write them down.

1.

2.

3.

Now think of a way you can get some scale or leverage from your offerings.

It could be working with five people at once rather than one person.

It could be something you invest in one time that allows you to make money long-term, like a new piece of equipment or software.

It could be as simple as hiring an employee and paying them less than what your time is worth.

Your Business:
A Game Changer for Your Money—
Action Plan Part Three

I n business, think of yourself as an investor. Every single thing you do in your business should generate some kind of return for you.

Think of your marketing expenses as investments, not expenses. You plant seeds, watch them grow, and then you get rewarded.

The money needs to come back to you. If you don't think you will get results that will ultimately fund your goal, then move on!

It's that simple. Simple until you stop investing in your business.

The minute you stop building, creating, and investing is the minute your business will just flatline. You won't make progress. You'll burn out.

And then it's kaputnicksville.

Write down three investments you're willing to make in your business right here:

1.

2.

3.

Now I want you to choose the investment that could give you the highest return for the money you invest.

I have created a PDF tool for you. It's called the Instant Raise Calculator. It's very easy to use. I even shot a video for you on how to use it. Just go to the resources tab to find out how you can get it.

Afterword

Money. You got this. Seriously.

This is your time. It's time for you to step up and create a financial life where you can finally breathe. And financially breathe.

It's not going to be easy. But if you chip away and make a little progress each day, you will be surprised at how far you have come.

It has been a joy to hang with you. Come back to this book. Pick it up. Open any page.

Then go take some action. Why? Because you totally got this! *Mwah!*

Resources:
Money. You Got This.
Bonuses

Thanks so much for reading all this money stuff!

Just go to this link to download all this stuff: www.jkrane.com/mymoney

As a reader of this book, I want to give you some free tools that you can use for your money life.

Want to work with me privately? From time to time I open up slots to work with me. Hop on my notification list. Go here: www.jkrane.com/workwithme

My free CD, "How to Grow Your Business and Have Fun While You're Doing It."

Check out my YouTube channel. Let's have some fun and learn some money stuff. It's at www.jkrane.com/youtube

- 5 simple wealth building strategies
- Mortgage Calculator—use this tool to determine how much of a mortgage you can afford based on how much money you make.

- Cash Flow Calculator—use this tool to take control of your money
- Spending-Savings Calculator—use this to track your spending. Find out where the money went, once and for all.
- Menu of Money—use this tool to plan how much money you want to make.
- Instant Raise Calculator—use this tool to calculate a potential return on investment. I use it to see if the expected return is worth the risk I am taking.
- Fund Your Goals Calculator—use this tool to calculate how long it could take you to fund your goal.
- How Much Money Calculator—use this tool to calculate how much money you need to save to fund your goal.

Disclosures

Information contained herein reflects Justin Krane's views and opinions as of the date of publication and is being provided for educational/informational purposes only; it should not be considered financial or investment advice or a recommendation to buy or sell any types of investments or insurance products.

Justin Krane's views are subject to change without notice. Some of the information provided in this book is from third-party sources believed to be reliable, but the information is not guaranteed. Mr. Krane and Krane Financial Solutions have not taken into account the investment objectives, financial situation, or particular needs of any reader; are not responsible for the consequences of any decisions or actions taken as a result of information provided in this book; and do not warrant or guarantee the accuracy or completeness of the information herein.

There is a risk of loss from investing in securities, including risk of loss of principal. Different types of investments involve varying degrees of risk, and there can be no assurance that any specific investment will be profitable or suitable for a particular investor's financial situation. Asset allocation and portfolio diversification cannot assure or guarantee better performance nor eliminate the risk of investment losses. Before making any investment decisions or changes to your financial situation, you should consult with your financial advisor and tax advisor.

Each individual circumstance is unique, and there is no guarantee that following any of the situations outlined in this book will have the same results. Past performance is no guarantee of future returns.

Any forward-looking statements or forecasts are based on assumptions, and actual results are expected to vary from any such statements or forecasts. No reliance should be placed on any such statements or forecasts when making any investment decision. The assumptions and projections displayed are estimates, hypothetical in nature, and meant to serve solely as a guideline. The results and analyses are not guarantees of future performance, and you should not rely solely on this information when making any investment decision.

Certain situations and examples outlined in this book are hypothetical and do not represent actual trading in an investment account. Individual performance will vary from any performance shown herein and may be higher or lower than the results depicted.

Hypothetical performance has inherent limitations, including the following: (1) the results do not reflect the results of actual trading, but are achieved by means of retroactive application, which may have been designed with the benefit of hindsight; (2) back-tested performance may not reflect the impact that any material market or economic factors might have had on the decision-making process had the investment been used during such period to actually manage investor assets; and (3) for various reasons (including the reasons indicated above), investors may have experienced investment results during corresponding time periods that were materially different from those portrayed. Back-tested performance does not represent actual performance and should not be interpreted as an indication of such performance.

Hypothetical information is provided for general informational purposes only and should not be considered investment advice or a recommendation to buy or sell any types of securities. The hypothetical results reflected herein are provided exclusively for educational/illustrative purposes only, and there is no guarantee that the hypothetical results presented can be achieved.

The information in this book is not meant to serve as investment, tax, or legal advice. Hypothetical results cannot know your exact individual circumstances, so consult an investment, tax, or legal professional if you would like more personal and comprehensive advice. In addition, your financial picture will likely change over time; therefore, it would be prudent to review your financial strategy periodically to ensure that it continues to fit your current circumstances. All examples are hypothetical and intended for illustrative/educational purposes only.

About the Author

Justin Krane, a financial life planner, is the founder of Krane Financial Solutions. Known for his simple, savvy, holistic approach to financial planning, he advises his clients on how to unite their money with their lives and businesses. He works with entrepreneurs to create a bigger vision for their businesses. Justin loves business strategy, and he is all about achieving business growth.

Justin believes that every business owner needs to know where they are with their business money. Using a unique system developed from his studies of financial psychology, he teaches business owners how to plan their cash flow and be strategic with their business finances.

Prior to founding Krane Financial Solutions, Justin was a vice president of investments and sales manager at UBS Financial Services Inc., in Beverly Hills, California, for 12 years.

Justin is a Certified Financial Planner™ professional. He received his Certified Investment Management Analyst (CIMA®) designation from Investment Management Consultants Association and in conjunction with The Wharton School of Business at the University of Pennsylvania.

He has been featured in *The Wall Street Journal*, *Entrepreneur* magazine, MSNBC, and CNN Money.

He is married, has three children, and lives with his family in Calabasas, California. An accomplished athlete, Justin was a former junior-ranked tennis player in Los Angeles. He loves to cook, travel, and speak Italian.

CPSIA information can be obtained at www.ICGtesting.com
Printed in the USA
BVOW08s1139051016

464222BV00001B/25/P